Community Corrections Acts for State and Local Partnerships

by Mary K. Shilton

This project was supported by Grant #91C1203 awarded by the National Institute of Corrections, U.S. Department of Justice. The information and opinions expressed in this document are those of the author and do not necessarily represent the official position of the U.S. Department of Justice.

Helen G. Corrothers, President
James A. Gondles, Jr., Executive Director
Patricia L. Poupore, Director of Communications
and Publications
Elizabeth Watts, Publications Managing Editor
Linda R. Acorn, Associate Editor

Cover graphic by Marty Pociask

"Compendium of Community Corrections Legislation in the
United States" prepared by Sandy Pearce and John Madler,
North Carolina Sentencing and Policy Advisory Commission

ISBN 0-929310-74-8

Printed in the United States of America by Mercury Press,
Rockville, Md.

This publication may be ordered from:

American Correctional Association
8025 Laurel Lakes Court
Laurel, Maryland 20707-5075
(301) 206-5059

Acknowledgments

This booklet is the result of a cooperative effort to provide an update on the development of community corrections legislation. It could not have been accomplished without the help of Don Murray of the National Association of Counties, who provided information about the role of counties as partners in community corrections. Mark Cunniff of the National Association of Criminal Justice Planners offered guidance about sentencing trends and coordination for successful community corrections. Anthony Travisono and James Gondles, Jr., of the American Correctional Association have guided the project throughout its development. Nolan Jones of the National Governors Association is to be thanked for his support and input about state contributions to community corrections. Jon Felde of the National Conference of State Legislators has assisted in providing information on state legislation. George Keiser and David Dillingham of the National Institute of Corrections are to be thanked for their assistance in guiding research for this booklet.

A number of correctional professionals have also spent hours reviewing this book. Among them are: Bobbie L. Huskey of the American Correctional Association; John O'Sullivan, Hennepin County, Minnesota; Robert Cushman, Santa Clara County, California; David Rooney, Dakota County, Minnesota; Dennis Schrantz, Office of Community Corrections, Michigan; Margot Lindsay, National Center for Citizen Participation in the Administration of Justice, Boston, Massachusetts; and Bruce McManus, Minnesota Department of Corrections. Sandy Pearce and John Madler of the North Carolina Sentencing Commission deserve credit for their support and assistance in exchanging information for this project. The author would also like to extend a special acknowledgment to Patrick D. McManus and Lynn Zeller Barclay, authors of the previously published *Community Corrections Act Technical Assistance Manual,* for their extensive contributions to the subject. The American Correctional Association expresses its appreciation to the National Institute of Corrections for its financial support of this technical assistance project.

Mary K. Shilton

Foreword

It has been almost twenty years since Minnesota passed the first community corrections act in 1973. Even before passage of the Minnesota Act, correctional experts and politicians debated the merits of its precursor, the California Probation Subsidy Act. The California Act represented the first serious attempt to influence local action in corrections through state subsidization. The advantages and the shortcomings of community corrections legislation in the United States have been widely publicized. Yet there have been few efforts to compare the essential characteristics of these laws.

What are community corrections acts? The American Correctional Association Task Force on Community Corrections Legislation defined a community corrections act as: "a statewide mechanism included in legislation whereby funds are granted to local units of government and community agencies to develop and deliver front-end alternative sanctions in lieu of incarceration" (Huskey 1984). This definition has been broadened in many states to now include sanctions in lieu of jail. Unless otherwise indicated in the text, the term "community corrections" is used in this monograph to refer to programs in community corrections act states. There are a number of other states that have not passed comprehensive community corrections acts but have undertaken community corrections programs through executive action and existing agencies.

Community corrections acts have come of age in the 1990s. A model community corrections act is under consideration by the American Bar Association. The number of states adopting legislation is steadily increasing. Why this interest in a complex state law designed to affect a variety of agencies and tasks? Community corrections offers a mechanism for breaking the mindless cycle of locking up more and more people in jails and prisons without first applying intermediate punishments. Aside from potential social values of community corrections programs, economic values are often cited as well. If crime and sentencing factors are held constant, some argue that states can reduce corrections spending because the cost of community corrections programs is less than prisons (National Committee on Community Corrections 1991). At a time when the United States' incarceration rate is among the highest in the world, states and local governments must carefully reassess their options and weigh the consequences.

The American Correctional Association has a long-standing commitment to improving corrections in this country; it began with prison reform issues in 1870. Its membership has steadily grown from prison administrators to an interdisciplinary group that includes members from each part of state and local correctional systems. The American Correctional Association has supported the development of community corrections programs for states and localities as part of a balanced approach to corrections. It has assisted in the development of professional education and standards for this discipline.

This booklet, which is directed to the attention of citizen advocates and decision makers concerned with the administration of justice, has been written to provide a comparison of how states and localities have implemented community corrections acts and programs. It is an update to ACA's 1983 publication on the subject and offers a comprehensive look at the lessons learned in the past decade.

This booklet points out the common and divergent characteristics of community corrections legislation in an attempt to present a range of options for states and localities. It does not describe community-based programs in states that have not adopted Community Corrections Acts.

Chapter I lists chronic problems confronting correctional systems and summarizes the impact of crime and sentencing patterns on incarcerative institutions and probation. It describes corrections acts as a response to pressures that influence the administration of state and local correctional programs in the United States.

Chapter II presents an analysis of common elements of state laws. The concept of community corrections is broad and can accommodate multiple goals and functions. States enacting such legislation have included various requirements in the legislation in order to influence correctional policy. As examples of this diversity, the common requirements of community corrections acts are outlined.

Chapter III summarizes what is required to implement an act. It lists typical steps to be taken in making the act work.

Chapter IV highlights the accomplishments of community corrections legislation. It presents an overview of the dynamic history of the acts and their benefits. Some barriers to successful programs are also noted.

Chapter V underscores the dynamic quality of community corrections acts. Maintaining the vitality of the legislation requires states and localities to continue to work together on a number of difficult issues.

An accompanying "Compendium of Community Corrections Legislation in the United States" reviews each participating state, highlighting the purposes, leadership, organizational structure, and administrative mechanism. This compendium offers specific information about the variations that exist in community corrections acts.

This booklet is not intended to offer a single model of community corrections for solving correctional problems. It suggests potential areas for state and local cooperative efforts to improve the administration of correctional programs in the United States.

James A. Gondles, Jr.
Executive Director
American Correctional Association

Contents

Acknowledgments iii

Foreword iv

Introduction viii

  I. The Motivation and a Legislative
     Response 1

 II. Designing the Act 15

III. Implementing the Act 25

IV. The Results 35

 V. Maintaining the Act's Vitality 42

Bibliography 49

Appendix: A Compendium of Community
    Corrections Legislation in the
    United States 51

Introduction

State correctional systems in the United States are unique among nations in their complexity and fragmented functions. Why should states want to pass community corrections legislation to further decentralize statewide corrections?

1. Most correctional functions are best performed in the area where the offender resides.
2. Community corrections acts offer a better way of handling responsibility for correctional programs through incentives for intergovernmental cooperation, public education, and local management of a range of sanctions.
3. Community corrections acts provide localities with an opportunity to engage citizens in the debate over correctional goals and in the allocation of scarce resources.

Community corrections acts emerged in the early 1970s as a reform movement directed toward rehabilitative programs. Since that time, at least eighteen states have passed community corrections acts. The motivations driving adoption of these acts are still relevant because these laws are flexible in meeting changed mandates.

What have community corrections acts accomplished? What community corrections acts do best is provide a forum to examine correctional policy, stimulate innovative solutions to problems, improve the administration of programs, and garner community support for them. Community corrections acts have improved professional standards. Some states credit them with providing a network for examining sentencing reforms. The list of measured benefits to the public, victims, offenders, and governments is growing.

States vary widely in how they have developed community corrections acts. This book highlights similarities and differences between state community corrections acts. Variations reflect different correctional philosophies, intergovernmental relations, resources, and politics of the states.

Despite wide differences, there is one common denominator: community corrections legislation shifts state funds and responsibility for correctional services from the states to localities, recognizing that localities can best manage policy and resources at the community level. The process of transferring funds and responsibilities to local governments requires a cooperative approach to management of correctional services. Cooperation cannot be achieved without a careful assessment of both state and local needs and a negotiated agreement between the parties. Local jurisdictions become involved in targeting resources to meet priorities. States become committed to assisting localities.

How can community corrections legislation help states and counties improve correctional services in the future? Community corrections acts have the potential to empower and mobilize communities to solve nagging problems of increasing numbers of nonviolent offenders. They provide a framework for systematically focusing correctional policy and resources, and they help improve systems planning and eliminate gaps in services. Once a community corrections act is operational, information can be gathered about the outcomes of correctional programs to better inform decision makers and the public. Thus, there are many reasons to consider developing and maintaining this legislation for solving problems within state correctional systems.

An earlier monograph, the *Community Corrections Act Technical Assistance Manual,* by Patrick D. McManus and Lynn Zeller Barclay, published by the American Correctional Association, provided the basis for this effort. The structure of this monograph closely follows the earlier publication with one major exception. Corrections in the United States is largely a shared responsibility of local and state governments. Community corrections acts are directed toward this joint responsibility. This booklet emphasizes the potential community interest in such laws.

I.

The Motivation and a Legislative Response

A Continuing Crisis In Corrections

Corrections in the 1990s is confronted by a host of complex problems that have stretched interagency relations to the breaking point. During the previous decade, the nation's prison population increased by almost 134 percent. As a result, in 1990 there were more than 1.2 million persons in U.S. prisons and jails. More than 670,000 persons were in state prisons. Another 408,000 were in local jails. This figure was exceeded by the number of persons on probation or parole during 1990. There were more than 2.5 million adults on probation in 1989, and 400,000 on parole (BJS 1990a).

These statistics resulted from unprecedented increases in the number of offenders entering the system. There were 4.1 million adults under correctional custody or supervision at the end of 1989 in the United States (BJS 1990a), one in every forty-six adults in this country. This represents since 1980 a population increase of 126 percent for probation, 107 percent for parole, and 114 percent for jails and prisons. Crowded jails, prisons, and probation and parole caseloads have increased costs and hampered corrections' ability to provide intended services. In 1991 more than $16 billion was spent on correctional services at all levels of government. In nearly every state, counties are responsible for providing adequate jail funding, and states are responsible for prisons. Funding responsibility for probation and parole services vary (slightly over half are now state-funded and just under half are locally funded).

Correctional expenditures have become the second largest spending item in state and local budgets due to increased needs for housing. For every dollar spent on construction, the estimated operating costs are sixteen times the costs of construction over the life of the facility. Despite a nationwide effort to build and staff more prisons and jails, states and counties have not been able to keep up with the demand. Most prisons and jails are over capacity.

In 1990 at least 28 percent of all local jurisdictions were under court order to limit the number of persons confined. Most state and federal prisons were operating in excess of their rated capacity (BJS 1991a).

Lack of space is only part of the problem. Unsafe or inhumane conditions exist in many prisons and jails. It is estimated that thirty-seven states are under court order for failing to provide adequate conditions. When courts set standards for prison and jail conditions, they frequently note the role played by crowding. There is growing awareness that scarce prison and jail space should be reserved for violent and career offenders. There is also an increasing recognition that jails and prisons are not the only places where people can be punished. Noninstitutional programs are more appropriate in certain instances.

The Advisory Commission on Intergovernmental Relations (ACIR) recommended that state and local partnerships be directed to solve the jail crisis (1984). The high cost of prisons and jails and the public's reluctance to spend more for them is one reason for a closer look at what community corrections acts can do to respond to crime. The high cost of incarceration limits what can be spent on the balance of correctional programs. In 1987 it was estimated that the cost of building a medium security prison was more than $61,000 per bed. Construction costs for jails were only slightly less than for prisons (Lauen 1990).

The most significant costs of an increasing rate of incarceration are the cumulative operating costs for prisons and jails. Operating costs vary with number of beds and security levels. According to one 1989 study, annual operating costs of prisons ranged from a low of $19,575 per bed to a high of $41,284 per bed. In addition to operational costs, there also are the opportunity costs of not funding other state or local projects.

Some argue that community corrections is a more cost-effective option. It costs $46.54 per day to house a federal inmate and an average of $54.79 per day to house a state inmate. These costs are compared with an average of $31.47 per day for halfway houses and $6.41 per day for home confinement with electronic monitoring (Way 1990). In Georgia, the cost of home confinement has been completely funded by offenders from supervision fees (Petersilia 1986).

Prisons and jails have been built in every state during the 1980s and should continue to be used to hold serious offenders who pose a threat to public safety. Although new facilities have been added, old ones are seldom closed. Population increases make it difficult to accommodate the capacity demand for prisons and jails. Two years after completion, new jails are often filled to capacity. Within five years they are 30 percent over capacity.

Increasingly, states and localities are motivated to adopt community corrections acts because of persistent jail and prison crowding problems. Community corrections acts are one part of a multifaceted strategy for helping address the prison and jail crowding crisis in a systematic way. One obvious method of alleviating the demand for construction is to reduce the number of people sent to jails and prisons. Community corrections states pay localities to provide a range of programs at reduced cost to the state. Such programs save institutional bed space for those inmates who constitute a threat to public safety or who require more intensive supervision than can be provided in noninstitutional programs.

Inadequate Funding

Efforts to handle the prison and jail crowding crisis are hampered by the rising costs of incarceration and supervision in the community, diminishing state and local revenues to support expanded programs, and interjurisdictional and interagency competition for scarce dollars.

Local governments take pride in their public safety, courts, and corrections services. However, in recent years capital expenditure projects have been limited. In 1991, the National Association of Counties (NACo) published results of a survey revealing the impact of budget shortfalls on counties (Zeldow and Gramp 1991). A majority of counties with populations over

1 million (52 percent) reported deficits. Counties with populations from 100,000 to 500,000 revealed a 39 percent rate of anticipated shortfalls. Many counties have cut back on capital expenditures such as jail construction and have made staff reductions across the board.

This situation is partly caused by the fact that federal assistance to counties declined by 73 percent from 1980 to 1986, requiring counties to provide additional monies for services for health care, crime, and drug problems. Nearly two-thirds of the counties increased their tax rates within the last three years. Six out of ten counties were not allowed to raise their property taxes, and many others reported state limits on sources of fees and taxes. NACo referred to these factors as a "structural fiscal gap." This gap has become one of the fundamental problems of running local government.

Fragmented Correctional Systems

The correctional crisis is an intergovernmental crisis that requires an intergovernmental response. The correctional system in the United States is not unified. It is divided into state, local, and federal services. Within each of these governmental levels are different functions and agencies. For example, probation may be administered by separate agencies housed within state and/or local governments and connected to the courts, corrections, or a separate agency.

More serious problems occur where multiple-agency services are needed for special needs populations such as the elderly, the infirm, or addicted offenders. For example, drug-addicted offenders or the mentally ill are often served by departments of mental health and substance abuse without input or coordination from corrections. Joint problem solving, local initiative, and interagency cooperation are required to provide effective services.

More than half the states have not yet designed a comprehensive strategy directed toward solving intergovernmental and interagency problems in corrections. Without a comprehensive strategy, fragmentation of the criminal justice system and competing state and local interests will continue to impede the development of effective correctional programs in communities.

The History

Community corrections legislation combines state subsidies and categorical grants to localities through a cooperative state/local administrative network. A *subsidy* is a transfer of money from the state to a locality. A *categorical grant* is an award of money to a local jurisdiction for a specified purpose. Community corrections acts are broader in scope than correctional subsidy programs or categorical grants. The additional elements include an administrative structure, comprehensive policy goals, program mandates, and the authority to carry them out.

Community corrections legislation attempts to relieve prison crowding, better manage correctional resources, and assure public safety by reintegrating offenders in the community. Many community corrections acts were designed to support programs stimulated by the Law Enforcement Assistance Administration during the 1970s. The first statewide legislation was adopted in California in 1966 as a probation subsidy. The need for community corrections reform was recognized in the Corrections Task Force of the President's Commission on Law Enforcement and the Administration of Justice in 1967. In 1973 Minnesota passed the first community corrections act.

The appeal for more humane, rehabilitative, and appropriate sanctions for nonviolent offenders gained momentum in the early 1970s as citizens, criminal justice professionals, and lawmakers recognized the need for offenders to have access to programs where they work and reside. Early programs emphasized treatment, work release, diversion, and decriminalization of certain offenses. Coalitions were formed that successfully lobbied for state legislation subsidizing community-based corrections.

During the 1980s, with a steady increase in the base number of incarcerated persons, the national mood toward offenders shifted away from rehabilitation toward punishment. The dynamics of community corrections reflected these trends as judges, elected officials, and citizens articulated a "get tough attitude." There were assertions that "nothing works" in rehabilitation. Community corrections programs began to emphasize punishment and offender accountability. Although less punitive programs remained part of the continuum of community corrections services, new programs addressed risk management, sanctions, drug testing, intensive probation, home confinement, electronic monitoring, and other alternative forms of punishment.

A Cooperative Approach

At least eighteen states have recognized the need for an intergovernmental solution by adopting a community corrections act, and others are in the process of considering legislation. Community corrections acts are designed to empower local governments to plan and implement community-based programs. They are state funding mechanisms intended to assist local governments to better manage correctional resources. States provide assistance, technical support, and standards to assure program effectiveness.

Agencies must reach a consensus about what is to be attained before engaging in problem solving. Community corrections legislation creates a structure for identifying shared values at the state and community levels. Once values are identified, a contractual relationship develops between states and participating units of government. The nature of the contractual relationship depends in part on administrative procedures as well as the forces at work in the state.

Reciprocal Duties

Community corrections acts transfer funds from states to local units of government to support a range of sanctions to be provided in a community where an offender resides. The overall purpose of this mechanism is to increase local options for non-dangerous offenders ranging from pretrial services to postconviction sanctions.

States and localities enter into a partnership based on a commitment to address complex problems. States retain certain functions. Table A reveals that states' duties are almost uniform under community corrections acts and provide authority to perform the following tasks:

- provide technical assistance
- coordinate training
- contract with localities and nonprofit organizations for services
- monitor programs

TABLE A
Community Corrections Acts—Comparison of Administrative Requirements/States

STATE	RESPONSIBLE STATE DEPT.	STATE ADVISORY BOARD REQUIRED	STATE PLAN REQUIRED	TECH. ASST.	TRAINING	CONTRACTING WITH LOCALITIES	MONITORING	SET RULES/ STANDARDS	APPLICATION PROCESS	PROVIDING PROGRAM INFORMATION	REVIEW PLANS/ PROGRAMS	HALT FUNDING NONCOMPLIANCE
				STATE RESPONSIBILITIES								
ALABAMA	D.O.C.	NO	NO	YES	YES	YES	YES	YES	YES	YES	YES	
ARIZONA	ADMIN OFFICE OF THE COURT	NO	NO	YES	YES	YES	YES	YES	YES	YES	YES	YES
COLORADO	***D.O.P.S.	NO	NO	YES	YES	YES	YES	YES	YES	YES	YES	YES
CONNECTICUT	D.O.C.	NO	YES	YES	NO	YES	YES	YES	YES	YES	YES	
FLORIDA	D.O.C.	NO	NO	YES	YES	YES	YES	YES	YES	YES	YES	
INDIANA	D.O.C.	NO	NO	YES	YES	YES	YES	YES	YES	YES	YES	YES
IOWA	D.O.C.	NO	NO	YES	YES	NO	YES	YES	YES	YES	YES	
KANSAS	D.O.C.	NO	NO	YES	YES	YES	YES	YES	YES	YES	YES	YES
MICHIGAN	****O.C.C.	YES	NO	YES	YES	YES	YES	YES	YES	YES	YES	YES
MINNESOTA	D.O.C.	NO	NO	YES	YES	YES	YES	YES	YES	YES	YES	YES
MONTANA	*****D.O.I	NO	NO	YES	YES	YES	YES	YES	YES	YES	YES	YES
NEW MEXICO	D.O.C.	YES	NO	YES	NO	NO	YES	YES	YES	YES	YES	YES
OHIO	D.O.C.	YES	NO	YES	YES	YES	YES	YES	YES	YES	YES	YES
OREGON	D.O.C.	YES	NO	YES	YES	YES	YES	YES	YES	YES	YES	YES
PENNSYLVANIA	******P.C.C.D	NO	NO	YES	YES	YES	YES	YES	YES	NO	YES	YES
TENNESSEE	D.O.C.	NO	NO	YES	YES	YES	YES	YES	YES	YES	YES	YES
TEXAS	**D.O.C.J.	YES	NO	YES	YES	YES	YES	YES	YES	YES	YES	YES
VIRGINIA	D.O.C.	YES	NO	YES	YES	YES	YES	YES	YES	YES	YES	YES

D.O.C.   DEPARTMENT OF CORRECTIONS
**D.O.C.J.   DEPARTMENT OF CRIMINAL JUSTICE
***D.O.P.S.   DEPARTMENT OF PUBLIC SAFETY
****O.C.C   OFFICE OF COMMUNITY CORRECTIONS
*****D.O.I.   DEPARTMENT OF INSTITUTIONS
******P.C.C.D.   PENNSYLVANIA COMMISSION ON CRIME AND DELINQUENCY

- publish rules and standards
- develop an application or planning process
- review application and plans
- conduct assessments and evaluations
- halt funding for noncompliance
- provide information to the public, decision makers, and professionals

Reciprocal duties include state duties of oversight and funding and local duties of developing and operating the programs. In most instances, counties provide correctional services. Some cities and multicounty areas are also designated as recipients. Several states permit nonprofit organizations to be direct recipients of assistance, particularly if counties do not participate.

Tables B and C indicate statutory requirements for local participation in community corrections acts. With some variations common local functions include the following:

- meeting specified plan or application requirements (e.g., public safety, data analysis, program analysis, application or plan submission, reduce commitments)
- observing funding restrictions (e.g., nonsupplantation, maintenance of effort, no construction funds)
- maintaining local advisory boards

Targeted Funding

Community corrections acts provide a mechanism for states and localities to compensate for the effects of two problems: (1) budget shortfalls and (2) imbalances in existing resource allocations.

Community corrections acts are designed to compensate for inadequate funding of local corrections by providing a budgeted state source of revenues. Some community corrections acts were enacted in response to a loss of federal and state funds under the Law Enforcement Assistance Administration (LEAA). Several states recognized the benefits derived from the LEAA grant program and continued correctional programs through a joint state and local subsidy.

Community corrections acts distribute state funds accord-

TABLE B
Community Corrections Acts—Comparison of Administrative Requirements/Localities

STATE	LOCAL UNIT PARTICIPATING COUNTY	CITY	COMBINATION	NONPROFIT	MANDATORY YES/NO	PLAN APPLICATION REQUIREMENTS REDUCE COMMITMENTS	SAFETY	DATA ANALYSIS	PROGRAM ANALYSIS	EVALUATION	APPLICATION	FUNDING RESTRICTIONS NONSUPPLANTATION MAINTAINING SPENDING LEVEL	LIMITS ON CONSTRUCTION	REIMBURSE LOCAL ADMINISTRATION COSTS	LOCAL BOARD REQUIRED? YES/NO
ALABAMA	YES	NO	YES	YES	NO	NO	NO	YES	YES	YES	YES	NO	NO	YES	YES
ARIZONA	YES	NO	NO	YES	NO	YES	YES	YES	YES	YES	YES	YES	JAILS	YES	NO***
COLORADO	YES	NO	YES/	YES	NO	NO	NO	NO	NO	NO	YES	NO	NO	YES	YES
CONNECTICUT	*	NO	NO	YES	NO	NO	NO	NO	NO	NO	YES	NO	NO	YES	NO
FLORIDA	YES	NO	NO	NO	NO	NO	YES	YES	YES	YES	YES	YES	NO	YES	YES
IOWA	NO	NO	**	NO	YES	NO	NO	NO	NO	NO	YES	NO	NO	YES	YES
INDIANA	YES	YES	YES	YES	NO	NO	NO	NO	YES	NO	YES	YES	JAILS	YES	YES
KANSAS	YES	NO	NO	NO	YES	YES	NO	YES	YES	YES	YES	YES	NO	YES	YES
MICHIGAN	YES	YES	YES	YES	NO	YES	YES	YES	YES	YES	YES	YES	NO	YES	YES
MINNESOTA	YES	YES	YES	NO	NO	NO	NO	YES	YES	YES	YES	YES	NO	YES LIMIT 10%	YES
MONTANA	YES	YES	YES	YES	NO	YES	YES	NO	NO	NO	YES	NO	NO	YES	NO***
NEW MEXICO	YES	YES	YES	NO	NO	NO	NO	NO	NO	NO	YES	NO	NO	YES	NO
OHIO	YES	YES	NO	NO	NO	YES	NO	YES	YES	YES	YES	YES	YES	YES	YES
OREGON	YES	NO	NO	YES	NO	YES	YES	YES	YES	YES	YES	YES	YES	YES	YES
PENNSYLVANIA	YES	NO	YES****	NO	NO	NO	YES	YES	YES	YES	YES	NO	YES	YES	YES
TENNESSEE	YES	NO	NO	NO	NO	NO	YES	YES	YES	YES	YES	YES	JAILS/PRISONS	YES	YES
TEXAS	YES	YES	YES	YES	NO	NO	NO	YES	YES	YES	YES	NO	NO	YES	YES
VIRGINIA	YES	YES	NO	NO	NO	NO	YES	YES	YES	YES	YES	NO	NO	YES	YES

* JUDICIAL DISTRICTS THROUGH COUNTIES
** STATEWIDE PROGRAM BY HEALTH SERVICE AREAS
*** LOCAL BOARD IS PERMITTED BUT NOT REQUIRED
**** COMBINED COUNTIES WITHIN A JUDICIAL DISTRICT

TABLE C
Community Corrections Legislation—Comparison of Resource Factors

STATES	LOCAL AID REQUIREMENTS					STATE FUNDED		USER FEES FINES
	PLANNING FUNDS	LOCAL MATCH	LOCAL MAINTENANCE OF EFFORT	CHARGEBACKS INCENTIVES	LOCAL FUNDING BASIS	STATEWIDE BUDGET	FISCAL YEAR	
ALABAMA	YES	NO	N/A	NO	N/A	N/A	N/A	YES
ARIZONA	YES	NO	NO	NO	BY APPLICATION	N/A	N/A	NO
COLORADO	YES	NO	NO	NO	FORMULA	$13 MILLION	1989-1990	NO
CONNECTICUT	NO	YES	NO	NO	BY APPLICATION	N/A	N/A	N/A
FLORIDA	YES	NO	YES	NO	FORMULA	$7.2 MILLION	1991	YES
INDIANA	YES	NO	YES	YES JUVENILES	FORMULA	$11 MILLION	1990-1991	YES
IOWA	YES	NO	NO	NO	FORMULA	$22 MILLION	1989-1990	YES
KANSAS	YES	NO	YES	NO	FORMULA	$4.1 MILLION	1989-1990	NO
MICHIGAN	YES 30%	NO	YES	YES JUVENILES	FORMULA	$19 MILLION	1990-1991	NO
MINNESOTA	YES	NO	YES	NO	FORMULA	$21 MILLION	1989-1990	NO
MONTANA	NO	NO	NO	NO	BY APPLICATION	N/A	N/A	YES
NEW MEXICO	YES 10%	YES	YES	NO	BY APPLICATION	$1.3 MILLION	1989-1990	NO
OHIO	YES 10%	NO	YES	NO	BY APPLICATION	$15 MILLION	1990-1991	NO
OREGON	YES	NO	YES	NO	FORMULA	$42 MILLION	1989-1990	YES
PENNSYLVANIA	YES	YES	YES	NO	FORMULA	NONE	1990-1991	NO
TENNESSEE	YES	NO	YES	NO	BY APPLICATION	$5 MILLION	1990-1991	YES
TEXAS	YES	NO	NO	NO	FORMULA	$50 MILLION	1990-1991	YES
VIRGINIA	YES	NO	NO	NO	FORMULA	$10 MILLION	1989-1990	YES

Note: N/A = NOT AVAILABLE

ing to need for correctional services statewide. This compensates for shortfalls in regions that have few resources but high numbers of offenders. It provides a method for overcoming structural funding barriers at the county level.

An Organized System

Lack of planning and coordination of justice functions has been cited as a problem in jail population management and court delays. In Oregon a governor's task force report on the state's program noted that planning should be improved to coordinate supply and demand for prison and jail space. The report's authors further noted that "Careful long range planning is essential to successful criminal justice policy and to restoring citizen confidence in the state's criminal justice system" (Governor's Task Force on Corrections Planning 1988). Long- and short-term planning are a result of community corrections legislation.

Offender characteristics can rapidly change, but through community corrections acts, a lag in services can be avoided. For example, between 1986 and 1988 the number of persons convicted of felony drug trafficking in state courts increased by more than 50 percent (BJS 1990b). During the late 1980s and 1990s, this increase in drug-related offenders placed additional demands on corrections. Drug-abusing offenders are now filling prisons and jails (BJS 1991b). About four out of ten jail inmates report using drugs (BJS 1991c). An increase in the rate of drug abusing offenders has placed additional demands on corrections to provide drug treatment and mental health services (Cunniff and Shilton 1991).

Through the community corrections act planning process, solutions are developed to meet the needs of a specific prison- or jail-bound population. For example, drug abusing offenders require treatment in a community or confined setting. Will existing substance abuse and mental health resources suffice, or will new services be required? Programs should be targeted to serve the population during each phase of supervision from pretrial to parole.

Community corrections acts provide a comprehensive framework to identify multiple problems and to tailor solutions. Improved planning and cooperation among correctional agencies is a precondition to providing an increased range of criminal sanctions for nonviolent offenders. Criminal justice services are coordinated among agencies represented on local community corrections boards. Planning assists in allocating more resources for difficult cases. (Resources can be either funding or other governmental services or facilities that can be brought to bear on the problem). Economies of scale and elimination of service duplication are benefits of improved planning.

Community corrections offers a structure for developing a wider range of intermediate sanctions for probationers involved in renewed criminal activity. These sanctions keep offenders under supervision in the community who would otherwise go to prison or jail. Supervising more offenders under probation in the community saves bed space, cuts costs, and meets offender needs.

The process for introducing intermediate sanctions to reduce reliance on prison has been extensively studied by the Center for Effective Public Policy. This effort has yielded a description of a policy-driven, data-informed process. To successfully implement intermediate sanctions, the following steps should be taken (McGarry 1990):

- provide an exact statement of why the jurisdiction needs intermediate sanctions
- articulate clear goals for sanctions
- create a range of sanctions driven by these goals
- collect and use information about the local correctional system

These steps have been further developed in a report by the Michigan Office of Community Corrections to outline the procedures necessary to accomplish them (1991). For example, the report recommends matching goals to populations by considering offender characteristics. Offenders are classified by whether they need prevention, early intervention, or diversion services. Characteristics of offenders are then used to develop eligibility criteria for program entry. Once the goals and eligible population are defined, services are developed to match needs. This is followed by an implementation strategy including:

- who will be responsible for determining policies
- what events must occur for the population to receive services

- to whom the services will be provided
- when and in what order events will occur in processing the cases (pretrial, postconviction, or probation)
- what the reasons are for this process and how they are met

The Michigan report notes that the complexity of implementing community corrections programs is one reason some have failed. Attention must be paid to the implementation process to build workable programs.

The following programs range from least intrusive to most intrusive sanctions:

Probation Services (generally rehabilitative) (least intrusive)
no conditions
probation with conditions and supervision
probation with treatment programs
probation with education programs
intensive probation with contacts
"split" sentencing with regular probation (short-term incarceration followed by probation)
intensive probation with drug/alcohol screening
intensive probation with split sentencing

Penalties, Restitution, and Fines (in conjunction with regular or intensive probation) (moderately intrusive)
victim restitution
community service
user fees
day fines

Monitoring
home confinement
electronic monitoring
drug/alcohol screening
day reporting centers with risk-control components

Residential Facilities (most intrusive)
work/education release centers
halfway houses
shock incarceration
jail and prison release centers

Community corrections acts provide a structure for monitoring program effectiveness and public safety. Aggregate risk analysis is a tool for classifying offenders, but it can be extended to secure compliance with sentences. Risk analysis is used to monitor offenders and to ensure conditions of release are met (O'Leary and Clear 1984).

Localities suffer the consequences of crime and eventually must take back most offenders with the hope that they will become productive, law-abiding citizens. Risk management issues are of mutual concern to correctional administrators and communities.

Community corrections acts provide an opportunity for public education and participation in correctional programs. Many citizens are not acquainted with the goals and functions of corrections. Public support for better funding of correctional programs is limited because offenders are perceived as less deserving than other groups. The result is often a reluctance to develop new community programs and adequately fund existing ones.

Professionals working in community corrections states report benefits from a network of service providers. Community corrections professionals have emerged as leaders in major state and national correctional organizations.

II.

Designing the Act

The Purposes

Community corrections acts are designed to transfer resources and funding to local governments to plan and implement decentralized corrections programs to better manage correctional resources. Increasingly the acts are intended to help relieve jail or prison crowding. The primary purpose is to create an administrative mechanism to support planning and coordination of locally operated corrections programs. By creating such a structure, community corrections acts institutionalize comprehensive planning and funding of corrections programs on a statewide basis. State laws are remarkably similar in goals but differ widely in implementation.

Goals are broad enough to permit localities to select options based on needs. Table D summarizes explicit statutory purposes set forth in community corrections acts. Among them are the following:

- offender accountability
- reducing institutional commitments
- developing offender supervision programs
- creating rehabilitative services
- broadening sentencing options
- planning and coordinating programs
- assuring public safety
- promoting cost effectiveness
- encouraging local involvement

All community corrections acts refer to program development in a community setting. Some states without community corrections acts have also adopted this goal through statewide

TABLE D
State Community Corrections Acts—Comparison of State Goals

| | COMMUNITY CORRECTIONS ACTS | | | | PURPOSES/STATUTORY GOALS | | | | | | | | |
State	Title	Citation	Enacted	Revised	Offender Account-ability	Reduce Institutional Commitments	Develop Programs	Create Rehabilitative Services	Broaden Sentencing Options	Planning/ Coordi-nation	Public Safety	Cost Effec-tiveness	Encourage Local Involvement
Alabama	Community Punishment and Correction Act	HB34	1991		YES	YES	YES	YES	YES	YES	YES	YES	YES
Arizona	Community Punishment Act	41-1604.07	1988	1990	YES	YES	YES	YES	YES	YES	YES	YES	YES
Colorado	Community Correctional Facilities and Programs	CO Rev. Statutes 17-27-10	1974	1977 1979 1983	NO	NO	YES	YES	YES	YES	NO	NO	NO
Connecticut	Community Correction Services	CT General Statutes 18-101(h)	1972	1973 1980 1982	NO	YES	YES	YES	NO	NO	NO	NO	NO
Florida	Community Partnership Act	FL Statutes 948.51	1991		YES	NO	YES	YES	YES	YES	YES	YES	YES
Indiana	Grants to Counties for Community Corrections	IN Code 11-12-2-1	1979	1981-1989	NO	YES	YES	YES	YES	YES	NO	NO	NO
Iowa	Community Based Correctional Program	IA Code 905.1	1977		NO	NO	YES	YES	YES	YES	NO	NO	NO
Kansas	Community Corrections Act	KS Statutes 75-52-90	1978	1980 1982 1989-1990	NO	YES	YES	YES	YES	NO	NO	NO	NO
Michigan	Community Correction Act	MI Laws 791.402	1988		YES	YES	YES	YES	YES	YES	YES	YES	YES
Minnesota	Community Corrections Act	MN Statutes Chapter 761 Sec 401.01	1971	1973 1977 1981-1983 1985-1986 1988	NO	YES	YES	YES	YES	YES	YES	YES	YES
Montana	Community Corrections Act	45-7-306, 46-18-201 MC	1991		YES	YES	YES	YES	YES	YES	YES	YES	YES
New Mexico	Adult Community Corrections Act	NM Statutes Sec 3-9-1	1983	1987-1989	YES	YES	YES	YES	NO	NO	YES	NO	NO
Ohio	Community Based Corrections	OH Rev Code Sec. 5149.30-37	1979	1990	NO	YES	YES	YES	NO	NO	NO	YES	NO
Oregon	Community Corrections Program Act	OR Statutes 423.500	1977	1979 1987 1989	NO	YES	YES	YES	YES	YES	YES	NO	YES
Pennsylvania	County Intermediate Punishment Act	Act No. 1990-193 61 PS sec 1101	1990		YES	NO	YES	YES	YES	NO	YES	YES	NO
Tennessee	TN Community Corrections Act	TN Code 40-36-101	1985	1987	YES	YES	YES	YES	YES	YES	YES	YES	YES
Texas	Community Justice Assistance	TX Statutes Art 42.13	1989		YES	NO	YES	NO	YES	NO	NO	YES	YES
Virginia	Community Diversion Incentive Act	Code of VA Sec 531-177	1990	1982 1983 1990	YES	YES	YES	YES	YES	YES	NO	YES	NO

corrections programs. In non-community corrections act states, it is rare to find shared state/local responsibility, comprehensive planning, and intensive program coordination.

Community corrections legislation increases options for punishing offenders. Offender accountability is implied in all statutes and is explicitly mentioned with references to "punishment" or "sanctions" in nine state laws. Legislation passed in Florida and Alabama in 1991, and in Texas in 1989, emphasizes punishment as a primary purpose of the legislation.

Community corrections acts offer a legislative framework for states to develop a wide range of sentencing options. While this goal is not always explicitly mentioned in the community corrections act, in many states it has been incorporated in program policies and priorities.

Caution should be used in relying primarily on community corrections acts to relieve prison and jail crowding. Although most states invoke this as a primary goal, community corrections acts are unlikely to solve prison and jail crowding problems without a comprehensive change in sentencing practices. The problem is often referred to as "widening the net," or filling up both jail beds and newly created community slots as well. Most community corrections acts are not designed to drastically change sentencing patterns, though they can divert nonviolent offenders to community programs. Community corrections acts can provide the impetus for carefully examining sentencing practices and developing methods for changing inappropriate sentencing of nonviolent offenders.

Despite this cautionary note, most community corrections legislation embraces reducing prison or jail commitments as a primary objective. At least fourteen state acts are directed to this end, and all community corrections states target their programs to decreasing the number of nonviolent offenders sent to prison. In Oregon and Virginia, evaluations have shown that commitments were controlled by community corrections act programs. However, in Oregon and Minnesota, an analysis of sentencing practices under community corrections acts prompted adoption of capacity-controlled sentencing guidelines. The adoption of these guidelines along with community corrections legislation represents an effort to provide both a systematic and a case-by-case method for reducing institutional commitments.

In its 1984 study of jails, the Advisory Commission on Intergovernmental Relations called on all states to adopt sentencing guidelines for both felony and serious misdemeanor offenders. Such guidelines should be based on legislatively predetermined population levels at the state and local levels. All community corrections acts operate under the assumption that public safety is a primary objective. Six states have public safety standards or reporting requirements incorporated within the legislation; most include references to public safety.

In designing community corrections legislation, states consider what public safety requirements they should meet. Public safety concerns address the following questions:

1. Should there be an effort to monitor and evaluate program safety?
2. To whom will this information be reported?
3. What authority will be vested in the agency with respect to public safety issues?
4. Will states or localities develop public safety standards?
5. What risk factors are most important to control in meeting public safety needs?
6. Are there adequate interjurisdictional and interagency efforts to track cases and share information?

Design of community corrections acts includes provisions for supporting the coordination and monitoring of programs to be funded under the act. Recognizing the need for planning and interagency cooperation is a significant part of most community corrections acts. States that do not have community corrections acts often lack a vehicle to sustain long-term program development and evaluation.

Nearly half of the statutes mention cost effectiveness of programs. The issue of cost effectiveness depends on many factors that are difficult to quantify. It is generally agreed that most community corrections programs cost less per capita than incarceration; however, few programs have been evaluated to ascertain that the intended target group is being addressed. This area needs more research to fully document the effect of community corrections programs.

The Minnesota evaluation of community corrections indicates that additional costs can occur. Local detention, if used as part of a community corrections program, can increase costs, as can local planning and administration. There is also a concern that community corrections will target a group of offenders who would have received unsupervised probation. These factors, together with use of community corrections programs for those who would have been assigned to probation, tend to increase costs unless carefully monitored. The design of community corrections legislation encourages local involvement in establishing correctional programs. The extent to which this purpose is developed depends in part on the politics, traditions, and values of the state. More than half the states explicitly recognize this purpose. Nearly all authorize local units of government to appoint community corrections advisory boards and recognize the need for citizen participation in program development.

Local involvement is important for comprehensive planning for community corrections programs. Once there is local involvement, community leaders, judges, and state and local correctional professionals can identify common problems to be addressed by the program. When counties realize the extent of their stake in developing solutions to correctional problems, they will be motivated to develop locally based programs.

The Scope

Community corrections acts vary in scope. They can be broad and address the entire spectrum of correctional services from pretrial to parole. A few states, such as Oregon, Michigan, and Minnesota, have sweeping community corrections acts. Others limit the scope to a defined group of offenders, outside of other state agency correctional programs.

Program scope can be specified in the statute or left to the cognizant agency and localities to articulate. Most legislatures have enumerated a range of intended programs to guide the cognizant agency. Options range in scope among the following broad categories:

- pretrial supervision and diversion
- probation and conditional release in the community
- intermediate sanctions and sentencing alternatives
- detention in the community
- parole supervision

In some states, counties decide which programs meet their needs and have flexibility to fund the highest priority programs. In other states, such as Kansas and Virginia, the state agency takes a lead role in determining which program priorities will be funded. In return for providing additional funding to counties, states expect counties to send fewer offenders to state institutions.

Elements

Before implementing community corrections acts, states and localities must carefully consider the following elements:

Goals. Community corrections acts should specify goals, such as reducing prison and jail populations or increasing local involvement in criminal justice programming. (See Table D.)

Offender eligibility. A target population must be identified. (See Table E.) Once an eligible population is identified, agencies can intervene with those offenders to better manage or rehabilitate them. Although most states target nonviolent offenders, several have left this issue open. For example, Colorado, Michigan, and Montana allow community boards to control which offenders are accepted into local programs.

Transfer of funds. Community corrections acts authorize a transfer of funds to local governments and private agencies for specified programs. The intent to allocate funding to participating units of government is a necessary part of the legislation.

Accountability. Localities administering community corrections programs are often held accountable through various performance indicators. Many states are developing information systems to allow them to monitor caseloads for consistency with the goals of the legislation. The use of data to monitor performance provides states, localities, judges, and legislators concerned with sentencing practices with periodic information on program impact. States undertake detailed analyses of sentenced populations to assure the target population is served. Chargebacks were introduced to reduce funds transferred to a jurisdiction if commitments to prisons exceed a set rate.

TABLE E
Community Corrections Acts—Comparison of Populations Served

State	Enacted	TARGET POPULATIONS			Felons	
		Juveniles	Adults	Misdemeanants	Violent	Nonviolent
Alabama	1991	YES	YES	YES	NO	YES
Arizona	1988	NO	YES	YES	YES	YES
Colorado	1974	NO	YES	YES	YES	YES
Connecticut	1972	NO	YES	YES	YES	YES
Florida	1991	NO	YES	YES	NO	YES
Indiana	1979	YES	YES	YES	NO	YES
Iowa	1977	NO	YES	YES	NO	YES
Kansas	1978	YES	YES	YES	YES	YES
Michigan	1988	NO	YES	YES	NO	YES
Minnesota	1971	YES	YES	YES	YES	YES
Montana	1991	NO	YES	NO	NO	YES
New Mexico	1983	NO	YES	NO	YES	YES
Ohio	1979	NO	YES	NO	NO	YES
Oregon	1977	NO	YES	NO	YES	YES
Pennsylvania	1990	NO	YES	YES	NO	YES
Tennessee	1985	NO	YES	NO	YES	YES
Texas	1989	NO	YES	YES	NO	YES
Virginia	1980	NO	YES	YES	NO	YES

Chargeback mechanisms focused on the rate of confinement of inmates to state institutions, as well as the services actually provided in the locality. Chargeback mechanisms represent an early effort to enforce the purposes of the legislation. The chargeback issue points to a lingering concern about how to design community corrections programs that achieve set goals. Chargebacks are controversial. Some contend they are effective in reducing commitments. On the other hand, localities argue that commitment rates reflect crime rates and judicial sentencing patterns—two factors localities cannot control. Chargebacks impede local participation because counties do not want to become embroiled in funding disputes.

Chargebacks have been completely rejected for adult programs. Minnesota and Indiana still use them for juvenile programs as an enforcement mechanism to ensure that community corrections acts have the desired impact. In most cases, they have been replaced with program monitoring and evaluation requirements geared toward effectiveness. (See Table C.)

Planning requirements. One of the unique features of community corrections acts is a system of local and state planning to set priorities (Tables C and D). Local planning requirements are included to identify needs and programs to be given priority for funding and technical assistance. Most states require local planning. There is less attention to statewide planning requirements in most acts. Statewide boards are not required in many states.

The planning or application process varies widely. With the advent of computerized information and classification systems, participating localities can provide detailed statistical data to state agencies. They can offer information on the demographics and risk characteristics of offenders in jails and entering the state corrections system. This detailed local information compiled by states provides an aggregate description of statewide corrections. It can be used, in addition to program monitoring and evaluation, for resource allocation, appropriation justification, and policy guidance. Recent state laws such as Montana's require that aggregate information be reported to state oversight bodies or the legislature.

Allocation mechanisms. Many statutes specify an annual allocation process. Others refer to a formula for calculating subsidy amounts as a way to divide the allocation among participants. Table C lists funding mechanisms. Most states consider local needs and available resources in calculating how the subsidy will be awarded to participants. The number of participating counties in some states is limited by allocation levels. In others, the funding formula is a source of tension between populated jurisdictions and rural areas. The allocation amount and distribution formula remain very difficult areas in community corrections administration.

Local participation. Local participation is primarily voluntary, although Kansas and Iowa mandate it. In states where local participation is voluntary, the state provides incentives for participation. Incentives must be substantial enough to outweigh the participation costs. In nonmandatory jurisdictions, recruiting and retaining counties hinge on negotiated agreements.

Participation can be phased, such as in Oregon, which has three optional participation levels. Localities can choose to provide their own probation and parole services or let the state perform this service. This graduated level of participation helps solve some of the problems between rural and metropolitan jurisdictions regarding subsidy levels and required services.

Funding restrictions. Restrictions on use of subsidy funds limit how localities can spend their monies. Limitations are an attempt to target funding for priority programs and assure compliance. In most states community corrections act funds have not been applied to build or renovate jails or detention centers. (See Table C.) In other states the funds cannot supplant existing local monies. Many states require localities to continue to fund correctional programs at existing levels (maintenance of effort) to receive additional community corrections funding. These limitations are designed to stimulate new or innovative programs for counties.

Counties argue that limitations discourage local participation and are sometimes inconsistent with a partnership strategy. Spending limitations withhold decision-making power from the counties. Power to control local correctional decisions is one of the most important incentives for county participation (Orrick 1988).

Michigan and Virginia have opted to let participating units fund programs to improve services for jail-bound inmates. Although many other states permit misdemeanants to be included in programs, most have not yet made a priority for jailed populations. The Michigan strategy is unique and deserves credit. It is based on an assessment that many persons now detained in jail are not dangerous and can be effectively sentenced to community programs. By removing nondangerous persons from jails, Michigan will attempt to save existing jail space for more serious offenders now sent to prison. This strategy recognizes the effects of a growing misdemeanant population on correctional systems and the potential of jails for holding less serious felons.

III.

Implementing the Act

Forging a Consensus

The work of community corrections depends on the nature of the problems to be solved and how they are approached by the proponents. The first step is to develop consensus about the mission of community corrections. Developing consensus and a broad base of support leads to improved outcomes for community corrections.

In a study of the forces behind the unification of community corrections, Nelson, Cushman, and Harlow found that unresolved problems within communities were a central driving force for change (1980). However, because of divergent views on how to solve these nagging problems, the problems themselves can present barriers to change. Educating citizens about the possibilities for improving a situation becomes essential for implementing community corrections.

Despite the enormous contribution of this analysis, more is needed to understand how the forces at work in setting up community corrections programs can be harnessed to achieve specific objectives. Information is needed on how correctional problems are identified and whether there is strong support for community corrections within a locality. Education about corrections programs can affect these forces.

Locally Defining the Mission

States that involve localities in the goal-setting process establish a mechanism for managing competing pressures on corrections. As noted in a publication by the National Conference of State Legislators, states and localities burdened by financial costs of supervising offenders lack the ability to render dispassionate decisions (Rosenthal 1989). Cost considerations are important but should not be the prime force in correctional decision making.

Citizens and counties should take the initiative in shaping community corrections from the grassroots level. The structure and management of programs stimulates local involvement. County and city priorities can be included in the list of statutory purposes for community corrections.

A community development approach has been suggested as a model for community corrections (Eynon 1989). This approach relies on organizing interested leaders to undertake programs to directly benefit the community. Once information on community needs becomes available, volunteers persuade local and state officials to undertake new programs. The impetus for community corrections comes from grassroots organizations, which start up programs using the department of corrections as a resource. Most state acts have not relied on a grassroots approach, but those that have done so experience less difficulty developing program roots.

The state can balance its objectives by setting funding priorities and negotiating shared objectives with localities. Mutual concerns must be significant enough to give both parties an incentive to form an ongoing partnership. Identifying mutual goals permits the development of a contractual relationship between a state and participating localities.

Linking the Mission to a Target Population

One of the objectives of community corrections acts is identifying the group of offenders to be served by its programs. Table E compares state target populations. Many states limit the program to nonviolent offenders or persons without a prior criminal history. An increasing number of states have amended their acts or guidelines to include jailed populations as well as prison-bound offenders. Some further limit intended population by listing priorities or programs to be funded.

Although most acts specify a target group of persons intended for community corrections programs, this is only the beginning of the process for selecting a population to be served. Sometimes the state targets a high-risk population to more effectively reduce inmates. The higher the risk taken, the greater the potential reduction in prison population. This must be balanced against local goals. Localities may limit groups of offenders to be retained in their areas. Montana and Colorado empower localities to make their own decision on who will be accepted. This tension between state and localities is resolved by carefully analyzing risk characteristics of the proposed group and providing adequate offender monitoring.

A continuing question for community corrections is whether misdemeanants should be targeted for the program. Some argue that they are unnecessarily jailed because they are not dangerous and can be more appropriately punished in community supervision programs. Others note they are never prison-bound and in many jurisdictions have already been diverted from jails. Statistical profiles of jail populations are useful in resolving these issues. An analysis of prison and jail populations should refer to the following information:

- number of offenders incarcerated in jail or prison
- characteristics of incarcerated populations, including the number and percent of inmates who committed nonviolent offenses or are classified as high-risk
- length of the average sentence for violent crimes
- length of the average sentence for nonviolent crimes
- number and percent of inmates confined for parole revocations
- number and percent confined for probation revocation
- average number of years revoked offenders serve
- whether revoked offenders violated a probation condition or were revoked due to an arrest or subsequent conviction
- jurisdictional variations in prisons and jail confinement rates
- jail and prison capacities and current populations, as well as planned expansions
- an analysis of jail populations by felons/misdemeanants, pretrial, posttrial, and state inmates being held while awaiting prison or sentence

After conducting a population analysis, a second step is to specify the types of offenders to be removed from jails and prisons. This involves a policy assessment regarding which inmates pose little threat to public safety when supervised in the community. This requires evaluating the characteristics of a given target group of offenders from other groups. For example, a group that is bound for probation may be first-time offenders charged with a single nonviolent offense and a history of full employment. On the other hand, prison-bound offenders may have a prior record, and may have committed more serious or multiple offenses. It can then be determined which types of services are appropriate. This process should be supported with data on the characteristics of various populations, their needs, and whether they can be targeted for prevention, early intervention, or diversion services. Judges and other public officials should be involved in making decisions about who can be safely released.

Once some agreement is reached regarding who poses little threat to safety, state agencies and localities need to develop risk management guidelines. These provide another method of managing risk for sentenced offenders in the community.

Other related target population issues are then resolved, such as whether jails or prison populations are given funding priority and whether legislation should address the need for assistance to both. Counties need to show substantial benefits from community corrections to justify participation. At the same time localities are seeking assistance, states are pressed to decrease prison populations. Without a reciprocal arrangement between a state and locality, either entity could be perceived by the other as "dumping" sentenced offenders.

One way to avoid complaints of "dumping" offenders is to develop a plan for intervention at each stage of the process, including pretrial diversion, sentencing, and postrelease supervision. For jailed populations, pretrial diversion programs offer substantial savings in case-processing and detention costs.

Re-examining Sentencing

Community corrections acts must be compatible with existing state sentencing laws. Some states have determinate or mandatory sentencing limiting the potential of increased sentencing options for a substantial number of offenders. For example, in New York state, a felon who is convicted of a second felony must be sent to prison. This sentencing requirement would limit community corrections to first-time felons in that state.

States such as Minnesota have reconciled sentencing laws with community corrections acts by passing sentencing guidelines legislation. Sentencing guidelines are one option designed to make sentencing practices compatible with state community corrections legislation. They re-examine available bed space and give priority to the most serious offenders.

Developing an Interagency Structure

Implementing an act requires consideration of the following issues regarding interagency involvement and structure:

- involvement of general purpose governments and their selected representatives at the state and local levels
- designation of a responsible state administrative agency
- specification of agency placement within or outside the department of corrections
- statement of the duties of the administrative agency
- indication of the relationship between community corrections and related agencies such as probation and parole
- specification of information and reporting requirements for the designated state agency or local agencies
- recognition of the responsibilities of state and local advisory boards
- selection of a state agency to receive and disburse funds

There is no set way to assign administrative responsibilities. The decisions will be based largely on local tradition, resources, and state laws. Whether it is a simple funding mechanism for local programs or a complex interagency network, the structure should be designed to achieve cooperation and consensus. Consensus takes time because actors must review proposals and develop policy in a group setting to ensure a wider sense of ownership of the program.

In every state except Michigan, Arizona, and Pennsylvania primary responsibility for administering the program is housed in the department of corrections. Although this approach has worked well in many jurisdictions, it does have some disadvantages. Michigan has determined that its agency will be independent from the state corrections department. Unless it has a strong commitment to community corrections, a state department of corrections is more likely to give budgetary priority to institutional needs when funding shortfalls occur. On the other hand, placing community corrections outside of the state corrections department has the disadvantage of lack of coordination or possible competition with corrections.

Gaining Interagency Cooperation and Planning

Evaluations of successful community corrections programs reveal they work best when there is interagency involvement. For this reason most state acts require or encourage local advisory boards. Connecticut and New Mexico are exceptions to this requirement, as shown in Table B. The functions of local advisory boards vary widely by state. In some states boards are required to submit a plan for systemwide community corrections. In other states, local boards submit a less detailed application and are responsible for setting policies on which offenders will be retained in community corrections programs. In some states local boards have authority for program development in conjunction with the county. In others programs must fall within a list of state priorities in order to receive funding.

Some states also have statewide community corrections advisory boards as listed in Table A. State advisory boards provide a general forum for correctional policy. They represent a balanced approach to community corrections and are representative of local interests as well as professional criminal justice interests. Judges, citizens, sheriffs, county representatives, and other service providers are generally appointed to these boards.

The authority of the responsible state agency ranges from highly involved to minimally involved in local program decisions. In some states, such as Kansas or Virginia, the responsible agency can refuse to fund programs that are not consistent with their priorities. In other states the allocation is given to the counties, and they decide what programs to fund. In Oregon, state oversight varies with participation level selected by a county.

Members of local community corrections boards include representatives of local government, law enforcement, corrections, prosecution, defense, the judiciary, and citizen groups. They bring with them their own views of what programs are needed in their communities. Boards require staff to research information needed for decisions. Local boards link parts of the justice system and the community.

Strengthening Local Responsibility

The state agency and participating localities achieve a balance in sharing responsibility. State concerns about local accountability and program outcomes will be satisfied by data collection and program monitoring. The state will need to reach consensus with localities on what results are to be expected and how data will be collected and interpreted. Localities should be involved in developing agreement on program accountability, goals, and outcomes.

Table F indicates how localities view benefits of participation. Benefits to units of government usually include greater control over programs for offenders. Counties need help developing programs to relieve jail crowding, offer drug treatment, and administer intermediate sanctions. Counties welcome the opportunity for better planning, coordinated management, and information systems as part of community corrections.

Part of the tension between states and localities revolves around two issues: who is accountable for results, and by whose goals the results are measured. These tensions can be overcome by detailed negotiations to establish common goals, acceptable measurements, and verifiable results. Negotiations should include the following concerns:

1. Are resources adequate?
2. Will program standards require additional expense?
3. Do counties have a say in developing programs, standards, and administrative requirements?
4. Will local responsibilities offer the potential for solving significant local problems in corrections?

Negotiations take time but can result in significant cost savings. If negotiations fail, mediation can be used to settle difficult issues.

Table F
Local Benefits and Costs for Participation

Benefits

1. Increased control over programs
2. Leverage CCA programs $ to support other county jail populations or misdemeanants
3. Improved coordination between state and local programs
4. Develop a local policy for sanctions and local probation/parole
5. Develop local autonomy/program
6. Relief of state prison or jail crowding
7. State resources are targeted to mandated services
8. State subsidy funds to localities
9. Local boards provide forum for problem solving/policy

Costs

1. Increased local workload
2. Locality may end up paying more for expanded services
3. State planning and administration requirements result in increased red tape
4. State parole/probation will run fewer programs, ship out sooner to localities
5. State attempts to divert $ decrease local autonomy
6. State cases may fill local jails
7. Reallocation of state resources may favor rural areas
8. Will state subsidy be sufficient to provide for costs? Will it be geared to increased costs?
9. State assistance may be important in problem solving, and state support may not be forthcoming

Providing Adequate Resources

Community corrections acts vary in impact on state and local budgets. Community corrections acts that rely heavily on punishments such as confinement and residential facilities tend to be more expensive than programs using nonresidential options. As the amount of contacts, supervision, or services increases per offender, so does the cost of the program. The financial impact will depend on the cost of supervision and the level of punishment to be required for appropriate sentencing. If crime and sentencing factors are held constant, some argue that states can reduce corrections spending because the cost of community programs is less than prisons (National Committee on Community Corrections 1991). Before states can realize savings, they must divert a large enough population to defer building a prison or to reduce the need to maintain an existing prison.

In contrast to potential state savings, community corrections acts are less likely to save counties money because counties' additional responsibilities for services are seldom fully reimbursed by the state. There are increased administrative costs charged to localities, and increased use of jail sentences, through use of split sentencing, can occur in conjunction with a community corrections program. This sentencing to local jails instead of prison can increase local costs of participation. According to a study in Minnesota by the Department of Corrections and the Minnesota Association of Counties, at the outset of the program in 1979 the state supplied $13.7 million and the counties contributed $23.3 million toward community corrections. By 1990 the county contributions increased to $71.9 million, while the state contributions increased only to $20.9 million. In short, over a ten-year period, the county contributions equaled more than three times the state share, underscoring the importance of county government in the overall program.

Many community corrections act counties have elected to participate and invest more county dollars because of local support for programs. These counties prefer to provide supervision rather than have offenders eventually released into the community unassisted and unsupervised. Offenders are encouraged to earn wages, pay taxes and fines, and support their families. Although state reimbursement to the counties must be substantial if the program is to succeed, factors such as local pride and creativity also play a large role in county decisions to participate.

Providing a Fair Formula

There is no easy way to divide available funds, but simplicity and fairness should be stressed. State agencies lack the resources to meet all funding requests. State funding mechanisms tend to use offender-based data including needs and risk factors as well as systems and workload data to determine funding allocations. Some of these data elements can be audited.

One source of tension states must often resolve is how they can meet the needs of their metropolitan and suburban jurisdictions while also providing assistance to rural areas. The following points should be considered:

1. Subsidy allocations should be fair and based on need. Urban jurisdictions with high crime or incarceration rates and limited resources should be given adequate assistance.

2. Local payments should be adequate to accomplish important but limited goals.
3. Some factors that can be used to develop formulas are: prison/jail admissions, felony sentences, parole and probation populations, cost of living, population, percent of population between ages eighteen and twenty-six, tax basis, and other indications of need or risk.
4. The formula should be based on verifiable and comparable data from all jurisdictions.
5. The funding allocation should keep pace with inflation and population shifts. A cost-of-living adjustment should be provided.

Gradually Expanding Services

Implementing a community corrections program requires giving consideration as to whether services will be available at each step in the corrections process. Not all services need to be within the community corrections system. Some may be provided by other independent but related agencies. If these independent services exist, they need to be coordinated with community corrections.

The range of services forms a continuum. The continuum extends from those requiring the least amount of supervision to those requiring confinement in a work release or detention center. They include the following:

- pretrial diversion, citation release, and pretrial intervention
- intermediate sanctions such as intensive supervision probation, community service, restitution, and fines
- monitoring, home confinement, and day reporting centers
- detention centers, shock incarceration, temporary parole/probation revocation centers, split sentencing, preparole release, substance abuse, mental health, reintegration programs, work release, and education release

Each locality can select from programs on this continuum or develop new and innovative programs. Flexibility in program development is an essential part of community corrections acts.

IV.

The Results

Accomplishments

Although every community corrections act state has published reports, Oregon, Minnesota, Virginia, and Kansas have issued the most extensive evaluations. The Oregon and Minnesota evaluations concluded that community corrections acts were beneficial and that improvements could be made through both legislative and administrative actions.

A series of evaluations in Minnesota covered: quality of services, efficiency, effectiveness, sentencing impact, planning, and administration (Minnesota Department of Corrections 1981). The Minnesota evaluations found no adverse impact on public safety. There were substantial improvements in planning and administration. Although per capita costs of offender services were reduced under community corrections in Minnesota, overall program costs were higher due to increased administrative costs. The benefits to sentencing practices were less than expected in Minnesota. Consequently, sentencing guidelines were developed to further structure sentencing discretion. Interagency cooperation, planning, and resource management in Minnesota were improved under the legislation. New services were developed in some jurisdictions.

A Governor's Task Force on Correctional Planning reviewed the Oregon experience and affirmed the validity of the original purposes of the legislation and substantiated benefits to participating jurisdictions (1988). The Oregon program was found to be effective but needed improvement in targeting state prison populations. The report recommended eliminating the chargeback, revising the block grant to more accurately reflect workload and costs, and adopting parole and sentencing guidelines. Since 1988, Oregon has modified its program to resolve a number of these problems. In 1989 Oregon adopted sentencing guidelines to further modify sentencing practices.

An evaluation of Kansas' community corrections act in 1987 indicated the program was moderately effective in retaining persons who would otherwise have been sentenced to prison. Recidivism was similar to those who were incarcerated. When compared with the cost of incarceration, the Kansas community corrections program revealed lower cost.

Examples of benefits in three states were summarized in a description of community corrections published by the Justice Fellowship (1988). The Justice Fellowship outlined the benefits noted in evaluations from Indiana (Gehm and Coates 1986), Virginia (Joint Legislative Audit Review Commission 1985), and Kansas (Kansas Department of Corrections 1986, 1987).

The following are some of the more tangible benefits of existing community corrections acts:

Victims

1. Victims were paid restitution by offenders. More than $88,000 was paid in Virginia between 1981 and 1984. Victim restitution in Kansas exceeded $361,000 in 1987.
2. Victim-offender reconciliation programs were part of community corrections programs in Indiana. In one Indiana county more than two-thirds of the cases were referred to this program.

Offenders

1. Kansas community corrections participants achieved a 95 percent employment rate in 1987.
2. Virginia offenders paid child support for their families while saving more than $21,000 in welfare payments.
3. Indiana offenders were offered education and employment services such as GED classes.

Community

1. A wide range of sanctions were developed in Kansas to meet jurisdictional needs. These ranged from increased supervision to job-readiness training.
2. Community service performed by Virginia offenders was worth more than $428,000. In Kansas, offenders

performed more than 21,000 hours of community service for governments and nonprofit agencies.

3. Supervision fees collected by Virginia totalled nearly $55,000. Kansas collected more than $250,000 in fees in 1987 to support administrative costs.

4. Kansas programs provided victim witness services to more than 6,100 victims of crime.

5. Supervision in community corrections programs meets public safety needs. Virginia and Minnesota reported that public safety was not endangered by the programs.

Government

1. Cost-effective supervision was provided in Kansas, where the annual cost per offender was less than $1,500, compared with more than $10,000 per offender in prison.

2. In Virginia, diversion of 142 offenders saved the state more than $325,000 in supervision fees.

3. In Kansas it was estimated that more than $30 million in prison and construction costs was saved by diverting 830 adults from prison.

4. The Virginia legislative study found improved planning among criminal justice system components through the community corrections program.

5. Economic losses due to offender unemployment and family disintegration were substantially reduced. In Virginia, offenders earned nearly $1.5 million in wages between 1981 and 1984. The benefits for continued employment and tax revenues were estimated to be even higher in Kansas.

Community corrections has increased professionalization of correctional services as local, state, and national organizations have developed training and guidelines for the programs. Among these are pretrial services, halfway houses, residential programs, community service, offender restitution programs, and probation and parole agencies. Community corrections acts have made it possible for service providers to define their professional goals and enhance their performance in community corrections act states. In some states professional training and conferences have been funded by community corrections act grants.

Why is professional growth an important accomplishment of community corrections acts? Community corrections acts allow decision making to be locally based with input from correctional professionals. Correctional professionals will manage the system and provide services once it is implemented. The work of community corrections professionals is specialized, technical, and complex.

A recent survey in Delaware indicated that more than two-thirds of the state's residents were in favor of alternative punishments (Doble 1991). Most people favored middle-level sanctions involving work over regular probation or prison. Reports from community corrections act states note the benefits of local involvement in introducing intermediate punishment programs into a community. Many citizens understand the purpose of these programs and favor a wider range of intermediate punishments.

Obstacles

During the past twenty years, community corrections legislation has encountered a number of obstacles. These barriers are caused by a combination of the following factors:

- forces at work in the jurisdictions and counties
- administrative or interagency problems
- legal problems related to the legislation or sentencing laws
- resource allocation or availability

Once the source of the impediment is identified, a coalition forms between relevant actors to remove the barrier through appropriate action. Such coalitions include state and local decision makers, citizen groups, criminal justice professionals, and judges. Some of the barriers that have been noted include the following factors:

Funding Problems

Because of state budget shortfalls, community corrections legislation in some states has encountered difficulty in securing adequate appropriations. Other states report cutting back on programs or declining to fund new initiatives. More than half of states surveyed in 1991 by the American Probation and Parole Association had experienced cutbacks in services (Reeves 1991).

There is a lag time of several years for implementation of local programs that are not already fully operational. Start-up delays can cause funding problems. New agencies with no track record for efficiency have a difficult time justifying their budgets. This can be remedied by a commitment in the statute to phased start-up funding for a new agency over a five-year period.

Few Studies of Results and Outcomes

After more than twenty years of community corrections, only a few states have published systematic evaluations describing what they have accomplished. The dearth of information about what works can be overcome by a concentrated effort to improve the quality of information about these programs.

Community corrections agencies need systems and case data to provide aggregate information on needs and cost to monitor their own functions. State legislatures, oversight agencies, and county boards are keenly interested in following the costs and learning the impact of such programs. There should be systematic reporting of services provided and problems encountered. Information can be used to develop minimal standards, to project whether there is a need for increased expenditures, and to determine whether the funding is targeting the intended group of offenders. Minimum standards for case management provide guidelines on the adequacy of correctional funding.

Unintended Sentencing Results

Although most community corrections acts have aimed to divert nonviolent offenders from prisons, this goal has been applied to a limited number of cases. Some state laws do not define the offender group to be targeted, leaving state agencies to grapple with this issue. If offender groups are not defined by statute, then study, rule making, education, and persuasion are necessary to carry out the program's intent (Pearce and Madler 1991).

Some programs operate outside of probation and are small due to limited funding or clients. There is a reluctance to develop programs to deal with more difficult offenders presenting correctional treatment needs such as drug-abuse or mental illness. Programs cannot possibly offset increased felony sentencing rates or enhanced punishments due to changes in state laws.

Offenders can be sentenced to jail as part of a community corrections sentence, causing jails to become crowded. Efforts can be made to prevent this result through judicial leadership and participation, sentencing guidelines, or administrative incentives. Community corrections programs increasingly have been used to serve jailed offenders as well as prison-bound offenders. Misdemeanants are not excluded in many statutes, although only a few states have concentrated on jail crowding issues. Michigan has taken the lead in making this a priority.

A third barrier occurs where more persons are sentenced to community corrections programs from a group who would have received unrestricted probation. This "widening of the net" may be due to the need for a wider range of options within probation, such as more intensive supervision. States such as Oregon and Minnesota have recognized this need and include probation as part of community corrections act programs.

Community corrections is not a solution to all sentencing and crowding problems. It introduces options for sentencing, but these need to be applied by judges. Community corrections requires judicial leadership and input for effective implementation. Judges are important members of advisory boards. If community corrections programs do not adequately reach an intended group of offenders, other mechanisms to reduce sentencing disparities should be considered such as capacity-driven sentencing guidelines.

Allocation Formula Disputes

Funding allocation criteria should be simple and verifiable. Allocation formulas should meet the basic needs of each participating jurisdiction. They provide funding based on needs for areas with high-risk populations. Workload and administrative costs are among the factors considered. If community corrections programs are intended to serve jail-bound as well as prison-bound groups, then jailed populations become part of the allocation formula.

A funding process should be open and well-documented to avoid controversy. Participating local units of government gain access to funding applications from other jurisdictions as well as basic information on what programs were funded.

Designating a State Agency

Finding an agency to house community corrections within a state can be a difficult task. The agency needs sufficient autonomy to do its job, yet it must be able to secure the cooperation of the department of corrections. Most agencies are within state departments of corrections. In Michigan, the legislature elected to make the office an independent agency autonomous from the department of corrections.

Program staff and stability are important to progress. Some states, such as Colorado, have had changes in designation of a state oversight agency to house community corrections. Whether the responsibility is assigned to the department of corrections, a criminal justice planning agency, or a separate department, implementors need to be certain related state agencies support the program.

Opposition to Administrative Requirements

Counties elect not to participate in community corrections programs if administrative requirements prove costly or difficult. For example, state data collection efforts fail if they require excessive amounts of information or data that is too costly to be retrieved. Efforts should be made to phase in reporting requirements over a long period of time. If counties are compensated for the additional costs to be incurred, they will be more willing to participate in the program. If they can meet administrative requirements, they will have more reason to participate.

Citizen Resistance

A new program placed in a neighborhood can face strong community resistance. Community corrections advisory boards provide a forum for considering details of the proposed program. Factual presentations augment an open decision-making process involving local officials, citizens, and neighborhood groups. Not all communities require public hearings, but such hearings offer a way to involve relevant groups and resolve concerns. Community control and support from civic leaders are important factors in overcoming resistance.

V.

Maintaining the Act's Vitality

Monitoring Program Effectiveness

Although community corrections acts have been in existence for more than twenty years, many questions about their effects remain. Some observers note that these acts' real potential remains undeveloped. The following are some still unanswered questions:

1. How do we know what works?
2. Will the legislation need to be revised periodically?
3. What methodology should be developed to support state and local efforts?
4. How can the state maintain its interests while encouraging local involvement?
5. How can information systems be used to better manage community corrections?
6. What are the prospects for improved professional services?
7. How can we continue to engage local support?

Many of these questions can be answered through the use of comparative data describing case outcomes and administrative costs.

Most states do not have data collection and analysis systems for cross-jurisdictional comparisons. Evaluations of community corrections have been generally favorable, but few have described case outcomes. Little documentation exists regarding increased economic productivity of offenders in community corrections. Likewise, there is little long-term data on what circumstances of supervision are more likely to reduce criminal activity. Are some correctional treatment modalities more effective for certain types of offenders? These are but a few of the questions needing careful research.

Revising Legislation to Fit Needs

The lack of systematic information about program success makes improving community corrections legislation difficult. Despite the absence of empirical information about program impact, states have frequently revised their statutes. Revisions have included the following:

- decreasing reliance on chargebacks as incentives for compliance
- changing target populations to include jailed offenders, misdemeanants, or juveniles
- changing county participation from voluntary to mandatory
- introducing wording to encourage local involvement
- designating a state agency to oversee the program

In addition to revising the legislation, community corrections acts need to be monitored for outcomes consistent with goals. Few states require reporting back on statewide outcomes and progress toward goals.

Updating State and Local Agreements

The success of community corrections depends on reciprocal state and local agreements, which must keep pace with rapidly occurring changes in corrections. This contractual relationship extends to each phase of the implementation process—from information collection to monitoring requirements.

The negotiated agreement includes not only program development responsibility and priorities, but also feedback on whether the act accomplishes its goals. Decision makers, correctional officials, and the public need to know safety-record and cost information. The state and the counties jointly develop the capacity to gather information required for monitoring programs under the act. This shared task depends on the ability of localities to take on an increasing workload of monitoring, reporting, and evaluating.

Limit Funding Restrictions to Necessary Functions

Most community corrections acts contain restrictions on how localities can use the funds. Typical restrictions include jail renovation or building, nonsupplantation of funds, and maintenance of effort. State agencies go well beyond these limitations in developing application requirements, reporting requirements, program standards, and priorities.

Table B lists statutory variations in funding restrictions, and Table C lists local aid requirements. There are substantial variations in maintenance of effort, local match, and construction. Chargebacks are now limited to two state juvenile programs. Many of these restrictions have been routinely required for state criminal justice grants and are a holdover from similar restrictions under the Law Enforcement Assistance Act. Continued restrictions show a state reluctance to let localities control programs. Although some controls are necessary, states should exercise restraint in controlling programs designed to encourage local involvement.

Although restrictions are intended to ensure the act meets its goals, they may have the reverse effect. For example, a county under court order for inappropriate jail conditions will not be able to afford to participate in a community corrections program that will take county funds away from improving jail conditions.

State standards and guidelines are developed to assure the program does what was intended; however, guidelines may also restrict county authority to revise programs or meet additional needs. Given competing considerations, a balance between state monitoring and county discretion can be reached. This is most easily done if counties are given a role in formulating the guidelines through a statewide task force or through a peer-review process using other counties and correctional administrators. Such task forces are at work in Michigan, Oregon, and other states.

Using Data for Improved Results

Community corrections systems are designed for flexibility in identifying new needs and providing solutions. Routine information is gathered to guide policy decisions at all levels of the program.

Programs must be designed to capture basic information, such as case characteristics, demographics, risk, and compliance rates. There also should be cost and systems information to analyze programs. Once this information is available, program personnel, local decision makers, and state corrections administrators will have a common reference for monitoring the programs.

Although data collection efforts may be uniform among jurisdictions, there will always be differing points of view in collecting and interpreting the data. State and local task forces can establish guidelines in this area. Data collection and use requires cooperation and consensus. Auditing data and confirming its validity are important tasks. Unless there is consensus on interpreting data, its use will be looked upon with suspicion. Therefore, mechanisms must exist for resolving conflicts related to interpretation and use. This should become part of an ongoing community corrections effort.

Data collection can become the first step in a multijurisdictional task to understand the outcomes of community corrections programs. The intent is not to collect a mass of aggregate data, but to retrieve information that can be used in guiding state and local policy decisions. In order to accomplish this, the data collection effort must be perceived as fair and reliable. The data should be easily and quickly retrievable. Aggregate data is directly related to statewide goals. Large numbers of variables should not be collected routinely; this can be expensive and will slow the process (Knapp 1991). Localities and the state agency must agree on the protocol for data collection and reporting requirements. After the data is collected, it should be audited for consistency. A task force or working group provides an ongoing structure for discussing the implications of the data for localities. If information indicates a program is not working, it should be reviewed immediately at the local level.

Engaging Local Support

One of the well-documented obstacles for implementing community corrections programs has been neighborhood resistance to program locations. Halfway houses and residential centers have been expensive to develop due to lengthy negotiations and difficult zoning requirements. Those who have studied this phenomenon emphasize the need to work with community leaders to provide information at each stage of the process.

Community corrections programs are more easily set up with the participation of local advisors and sponsors. These sponsors help inform the public about the safety of local programs. They become advocates for new programs to meet local needs. They participate in discussions about neighborhood concerns and help establish guidelines for what types of cases can be accepted in local programs. There must be a mechanism for hearing their concerns and a commitment to providing information on the safety of the program. Public meetings and information should target the following:

- what punishments are considered and why they are punishments
- what risk management procedures will be used
- whether the risk management program will be effective
- how these programs will affect tax rates or local services
- what methods of monitoring programs will be used, and what the evaluation methods will be
- who will decide whether a program will continue
- how implementors plan to handle public concerns throughout the life of the program (Lindsay 1989)

Maintaining Local Boards

Local advisory boards provide a forum for engaging public support. There are two types of boards: those that are responsible for planning or developing an application under a community corrections act, and those that are advisory to public officials such as a chief probation officer or a state agency. Board members are elected officials and citizen representatives as well as judges and correctional professionals. Local boards operating under most community corrections acts are required to report to a county or regional entity. Their work focuses on upgrading their jurisdiction's ability to provide correctional supervision for nonviolent offenders outside of prison or jail by developing a range of sanctions.

Local boards perform a range of functions, including program development and planning, public education, program monitoring, setting eligibility standards, and coordinating service delivery. They provide a commitment of funding and/or other resources to the effort. They can garner assistance from other systems, such as mental health services. Advisory groups provide for renewed citizen interest and support in community corrections programs.

The Life Cycle of Community Corrections and Rejuvenation

Community corrections programs tend to have a "life cycle" with a predictable series of dynamics. A review of the history of early legislation in California, Minnesota, and Oregon reveals that there have been dynamic changes in these programs, some of which can be attributed to the dynamics of correctional reform.

Once a community corrections act is in place, citizen advocates and reform-minded decision makers tend to defer to correctional administrators, planners, and program directors. Planners and correctional professionals influence the "middle age" of community corrections more than the reformers who stimulated the original legislation. Community corrections legislation in mid-life tends to become limited by its own efforts to stabilize and institutionalize local correctional services. This is quite understandable given the complex task assigned to community corrections and the limited resources.

States with community corrections acts assure the vitality of the act with continued funding, an engaged citizenry, and committed counties. How can community corrections maintain its initial thrust to decentralize and improve citizen involvement? Two points are critical. First, systematic information must be provided to the public and decision makers based on real data and results. Second, local citizen boards must have access to this information for making policy recommendations to corrections professionals and counties. These boards form a link to citizens about local concerns, a forum for discussing new strategies, and a linkage with community values. Unless this process of public education continues to take place, community corrections will fail to accomplish one of its goals—providing locally based support.

Conclusion

The impetus for most community corrections acts stems from a legislative policy commitment to develop alternative sentencing options and to deinstitutionalize nondangerous incarcerated persons. This intent is incorporated in the language of the statutes governing community corrections. The real promise for community corrections acts is to provide better interagency cooperation, citizen education, and community management of correctional programs for sentenced offenders. The history of community corrections demonstrates its potential as a problem-solving tool of the 1990s.

Community corrections acts have a different impact on each state. Evaluations indicate the effectiveness of programs funded by community corrections acts. However, with the increasing problems confronting corrections, the driving need to provide adequate correctional services becomes a dominant factor in implementing programs. Improving community corrections acts depends on a close analysis of sentenced populations and their needs. Establishing a continuing connection with the community is an important factor for success. State legislation will be useful to the extent that it enables states and localities to become partners in corrections. These partnerships must be based on a better understanding of offender needs and services.

Bibliography

Advisory Commission on Intergovernmental Relations. 1984. *Jails: Intergovernmental dimensions of a local problem.* Washington, D.C.

Bureau of Justice Statistics. November 1990. *Probation and parole 1989.* Washington, D.C.: U.S. Department of Justice.

Bureau of Justice Statistics. December 1990. *Felony sentences in state courts, 1988.* Washington, D.C.: U.S. Department of Justice.

Bureau of Justice Statistics. June 1991. *Jail inmates, 1990.* Washington, D.C.: U.S. Department of Justice.

Bureau of Justice Statistics. 1991. *National update.* Washington, D.C.: U.S. Department of Justice.

Bureau of Justice Statistics. April 1991. *Profile of jail inmates, 1989.* Washington, D.C.: U.S. Department of Justice.

Cunniff, Mark A., and Mary K. Shilton. 1991. *Variations on felony probation.* Washington, D.C.: The National Association of Criminal Justice Planners.

Doble, John. 1991. *Punishing criminals: The people of Delaware consider the options.* Public Agenda Foundation.

Eynon, Thomas G. 1989. Building community support. *Corrections Today* (April).

Gehm, John, and Robert B. Coates. 1986. The Indiana community corrections act process, practice, and implications. In: *PACT Institute of Justice.*

Governor's Task Force on Corrections Planning. 1988. *A strategic corrections plan for Oregon: Restoring the balance.* Final report of the Oregon jail overcrowding project. Salem, Ore.

Huskey, Bobbie L. 1984. Community corrections acts help promote community based learning. *Corrections Today* (February).

Joint Legislative Audit Review Commission. 1985. *The community diversion incentive program of the Virginia Department of Corrections.* Richmond, Va.: Commonwealth of Virginia.

Justice Fellowship. September 1988. *Justice fellowship program description, community corrections act.*

Kansas Department of Corrections. 1987. *Kansas Department of Corrections annual report on community corrections.*

Kansas Department of Corrections, Community Services Division. 1986. *Community corrections progress report.* (July).

Knapp, Kay. August 1991. Unpublished presentation. Center for Rational Public Policy.

Lauen, Roger J. 1990. *Community-managed corrections.* Second edition. Laurel, Md.: American Correctional Association.

Lindsay, Margot C. 1989. *Journal of the National Prison Project* (Fall).

McGarry, Peggy. 1990. Improving the use of intermediate sanctions. *Community Corrections Quarterly.* (Spring).

Michigan Office of Community Corrections. December 1991. *The management of diversion programs in the Michigan corrections system: A call for rationality.*

Minnesota Department of Corrections. January 1981. *Minnesota community corrections act evaluation.* St. Paul, Minn.

National Committee on Community Corrections. 1991. Position paper. Washington, D.C.

Nelson, E.K., Jr., Robert Cushman, and Nora Harlow. 1980. *Program models: Unification of community corrections.* Washington, D.C.: U.S. Department of Justice, National Institute of Justice.

O'Leary, Vincent, and Todd Clear. 1984. *Directions for community corrections in the 1990s.* Washington, D.C.: National Institute of Corrections.

Orrick, Kelly. 1988. What is in it for the counties? *County News.*

Pearce, Sandy, and John Madler. 1991. *A compendium of community corrections legislation in the United States.* North Carolina Sentencing and Policy Advisory Commission.

Petersilia, Joan. 1986. Exploring the option of house arrest. *Federal Probation.* (June).

Reeves, Rhonda. 1991. Down, but not out. *Perspectives* (Fall).

Rosenthal, Cindy Simon. 1989. *Opportunities in community corrections.* National Conference of State Legislators.

Way, Cory T. 1990. *Punishment without bars: Community corrections in the Federal Bureau of Prisons.* Senior thesis. Princeton, N.J.: Princeton University.

Zeldow, Frederic, and Kathleen Gramp. August 1991. *County government budget shortfall report.* Washington, D.C.: National Association of Counties.

Appendix

A Compendium of Community Corrections Legislation in the United States

Prepared by:
Sandy Pearce, Associate Director
John Madler, Research Associate
North Carolina Sentencing and Policy Advisory
  Commission

November 1991

Alabama Community Punishment and Corrections Act

Purpose: In 1991, Alabama passed a voluntary Community Punishment and Corrections Act (CPCA). The purpose of the act is to provide alternatives to incarceration (jail and prison) in the community for nonviolent offenders. However, due to the state's financial condition, no funds were appropriated to implement the act.

Impetus/Leadership: The impetus for enacting the Community Punishment and Corrections Act was prison crowding. Leadership for enacting the CPCA came from the executive branch, specifically the Secretary of the Department of Corrections. The bill was originally introduced in 1990, but it failed to gain support in the legislature. Defense attorneys were concerned about liability clauses in the bill, and it died in committee. However, administration officials worked hard to build a consensus for supporting the bill, and it passed in 1991 with the support of the County Commissioners Association, district attorneys, and defense attorneys.

Organizational Structure: In Alabama, the Department of Corrections administers adult institutions, work release centers, the Supervised Intensive Restitution Program, and jail inspections. The State Board of Pardons and Paroles grants paroles and provides a statewide system of adult felony probation and parole services. The Administrative Office of the Courts administers misdemeanor probation and parole services.

Administration: Alabama passed the Community Punishment and Corrections Act in July 1991, and it became effective 1 October 1991. The Department of Corrections has responsibility for administering the act; however, no funds were provided to administer or implement the act. State staff provide technical assistance to counties to apply for funds, to review and award contracts for grants, to monitor program performance, and to develop program standards.

Fundable Programs: Community Punishment and Corrections Act funds may be used to develop or expand the range of community punishments and services at the local level. Fundable programs include: day reporting, home detention, restitution programs, community service supervision, short-term residential treatment, individualized services that provide evaluation and treatment for special needs offenders, and substance abuse programs. Violent offenders are excluded from participation in CPCA programs.

Application Process: The Department of Corrections is required to develop and implement an application process for CPCA funds. In order to qualify for funds, judicial circuits or counties must form local community punishment and corrections planning boards and submit local plans. The state can contract with counties or with nonprofit entities to provide services prescribed by local plans.

Funding Formula/State Appropriations: No funding formula is specified in the legislation. In 1991, no funds were appropriated to implement the Community Punishment and Corrections Act.

Arizona Community Punishment Program

Purpose: In 1988, Arizona passed the Community Punishment Program; however, they did not appropriate any funds for it during the first year. The original purpose of the program was to provide services to enhance probation. The legislature has since changed the primary emphasis to prison and jail diversion.

Any person for whom a presentence report is ordered or any person placed on supervised probation or intensive probation by a participating superior court is eligible to receive services offered in a community punishment program.

Impetus/Leadership: Representatives of the local community, Justice Fellowship, and some of the state's judges provided the impetus for the Community Punishment Program. Their goal was to discuss ways to develop and expand community-based treatment for adults on probation. More recently the legislature has taken the lead by mandating annual diversion goals.

Organizational Structure: The Department of Corrections administers adult institutions and parole services. The Board of Pardons and Paroles, which paroles adults, is an independent agency reporting to the governor. The Administrative Office of the Courts (AOC) administers adult and juvenile probation services and the Community Punishment Program. The AOC administers probation services through county probation offices.

Administration: The Administrative Office of the Courts administers the Community Punishment Program through its Adult Services Division. The division is responsible for administering the state funds and for prescribing the procedures, guidelines, forms, standards, and requirements. The guidelines are promulgated through judicial order rather than legislation. The division also monitors local programs through inspections and audits.

The central office consists of a small staff that approves plans submitted by the counties, makes appropriation requests of the legislature, and distributes the funds to the county offices. The superior courts develop annual plans and funding requests, and contract with the local service providers. The court may, but is not required to, appoint a community punishment advisory committee to assess needs and make recommendations. The administrative budget is approximately $150,000 per fiscal year.

Fundable Programs: Community Punishment Program funds can be used for a variety of programs depending on the needs of the community. Examples include treatment programs for sex offenders and for the chronically mentally ill, community residential programs, substance abuse counselors on the probation staff, drug intervention programs, substituting community service hours for jail days, work furlough programs, and electronic monitoring using visual telephones. The emphasis of each program, however, is to be on treatment or jail reduction.

Application Process: Superior courts, sometimes with recommendations from a community punishment advisory committee, develop annual program plans with funding requests. The plan should include defined goals and objectives for the program, data to be collected and retained for evaluation and review of the program, and program component priorities in case of insufficient funds. These plans are submitted to the central office. The central office reviews the plans and gives final approval, and makes the appropriation request. Participation is voluntary, and as of November 1991, six of fifteen counties participated.

Funding Formula/State Appropriation: Arizona does not currently use a funding formula. The intention is to allow counties to diversify services as needed in the community. The only restriction is that the program plan must meet division approval. The state appropriates $2.5 million annually for the Community Punishment Program, $10 million for intensive probation, and $10 million for regular probation.

Colorado Community Corrections Act

Purpose: In 1974, Colorado passed the Community Corrections Act; however, no funds were appropriated that year.

The initial purpose of the act was to expand options for the courts and the criminal justice system to divert certain prison-bound offenders. The legislature has added the prevention of the expansion of the prison population as a purpose.

Originally the act targeted nonviolent felony offenders convicted of certain classes of offenses, which are primarily property offenses. Several years after the establishment of the act, the legislature added to the targeted population the transition of inmates prior to release to parole or as a condition of parole.

Impetus/Leadership: State legislators and locally elected officials provided the leadership for getting the Community Corrections Act passed. They were concerned with expanding the diversion options for the criminal justice system within the community, with managing populations that would otherwise be placed in secure facilities, and with increasing local control over correctional programs. The criminal justice system was very cooperative and welcomed the new options.

Organizational Structure: The Department of Corrections administers adult corrections. The Board of Parole is an independent agency which grants parole to adults, but the Division of Community Services in the Department of Corrections administers parole supervision. The Judicial Department administers adult and juvenile probation services. The Department of Public Safety (DPS) administers the Community Corrections Act programs.

Administration: The DPS administers the Community Corrections Act programs. The staff at the state level consists of six people. They contract with local boards to provide services, deal with the legislature and the governor, promulgate standards, perform audits in conjunction with local officials, and maintain a statewide database on all clients for evaluation purposes.

The local community corrections boards develop the service plans to submit to DPS, and they retain the final right to accept or reject offenders whom they feel they cannot properly serve.

Fundable Programs: Community Corrections Act funds may be used to fund almost any type of program; however, the DPS does have a list of minimum services the county is required to provide with CCA funds. These services may be residential, but they must provide drug testing, substance abuse and mental health treatment options, employment assistance, and family and financial counseling. Counties may also spend a portion of the funds for programs in jails. The boards are permitted to keep up to 5 percent of the state funds for administrative costs.

Application Process: To be eligible for Community Corrections Act funds, the county commissioners must create a community corrections board. The board may be advisory or functional, at the discretion of the county authorities. The board develops a plan for providing local services. The board submits the plan to the DPS, which has final approval over every plan. The department then contracts with the board to provide the services. The board contracts locally for the services.

Funding Formula/State Appropriation: Funding is based on an analysis of the caseload in the county. The legislature appropriates money to two funds: one for programs for inmates and one for programs for probationers. The Department of Public Safety then distributes the money from each fund to the counties based on the results of the analysis. Funds are distributed at the beginning of each quarter to the community corrections boards for them to disperse as necessary.

The Colorado legislature appropriates $21 million annually for the Community Corrections Act programs.

Connecticut Community Corrections Services Act

Purpose: In 1980, Connecticut passed the Community Corrections Services Act. The purpose of the act is to provide noninstitutional community-based service programs for prison and jail inmates upon their release. The act targets paroled inmates only.

Impetus/Leadership: In 1971, a network of private sector criminal justice providers existed in Connecticut. The Department of Correction selected them because they already had stability and stature, and developed them into an organized constituency to educate the public and the legislature on criminal justice system issues. They hoped to turn these issues into public policy issues to be discussed openly and rationally, rather than continuing to deal with them emotionally. The efforts of these private sector providers, with the support of the Department of Correction, resulted in the passing of the Community Corrections Services Act.

Organizational Structure: The Connecticut correctional system contains the Department of Correction, which administers adult institutions; the Department of Children and Youth Services, which administers juvenile institutions and aftercare services; and the Judicial Department, Family Division, which administers juvenile probation. The Department of Correction is divided into the Division of Institution Services, the Division of Community Services, the Division of Inmate Classification Services, the Division of Parole, and the Office of Adult Probation. The Parole Board is an autonomous agency with its members appointed by the governor. There is a Prison and Jail Overcrowding Commission which makes policy recommendations. As of 1 January 1991, the legislature created an Office of Alternative Sanctions in the Judicial Department. This office will gradually assume the pretrial and probation programs currently under the DOC. The entire system, including jails, is state-administered and state-funded.

Administration: The Division of Community Services within the Department of Correction administers the Community Corrections Services Act. The department is solely responsible for negotiating the independent contracts with the private sector providers, and monitoring and evaluating the programs and their impact.

Fundable Programs: Community Corrections Services funds can be used to cover the entire continuum of early release programs for offenders, both residential and nonresidential. The emphasis is on preparing the offender to reenter society, including such aspects as job placement, treatment, counseling, and housing.

Application Process: The state is divided into community corrections service areas, which correspond to health systems agency regions. The Department of Correction develops and revises annually a comprehensive state community correction plan for the delivery of services in the service areas. The community provides input, but there is no formal local advisory board.

Funding Formula/State Appropriation: Currently, the Department of Correction does not use a funding formula. The Department pays the money up-front annually on more than fifty private independent contracts. During this fiscal year, the department intends to examine the current contracts to determine how much it is paying for what services and thereby develop a formula for establishing the level of funds for each service area and for each service contract. This formula should include: (1) private sector match; (2) client population ratio; (3) nonclient criteria; (4) residential facility criteria; and (5) nonresidential facility criteria.

In fiscal year 1990, the legislature appropriated $15 million for Community Corrections Services and $7 million for Alternative Sanctions.

Impact Evaluations: No one has performed a thorough evaluation, but limited studies have shown that the more intensive, primarily residential programs have been more beneficial to the parolees than the less intensive ones.

Florida Community Corrections Act

Purpose: In July 1991, Florida passed a voluntary Community Corrections Partnership Act (CCPA). The purpose of the act is to divert nonviolent offenders from the state prison system by punishing these offenders with community-based sanctions. The intent is to reserve the state prison system for offenders who are deemed most dangerous to the community. For counties that participate in the partnership, an additional purpose is to reduce the number of nonviolent misdemeanants committed to the county detention system. Counties are to use act resources for intermediate sanctions for prison-bound or jail-bound offenders.

Impetus/Leadership: The executive branch provided the impetus for the Community Corrections Partnership Act—specifically the governor's office. It took two years to pass the act. Staff from the governor's office worked closely with the Sheriffs' Association and the Association of County Commissioners to gain support for the bill in the legislature. The State of Florida had been committed to community-based sanctions for several years and the CCPA was an expansion of that philosophy.

Organizational Structure: The Florida Department of Corrections provides a decentralized correctional system for adult offenders. Institutional and felony probation and parole services are administered on a regional basis. Regional directors are responsible to the Secretary of the department. In addition to regular felony probation and parole supervision, the Department of Corrections administers a community control program (house arrest), intensive drug offender probation, a statewide pretrial intervention (release) program, and restitution centers.

The Department of Corrections is also responsible for monitoring local jails for adherence to state standards. The Probation and Parole Commission, an autonomous agency, is responsible for making decisions concerning the release of adults on parole.

Persons tried as adults for felony offenses and sentenced to one or more years are committed to the custody of the Department of Corrections. Persons tried and sentenced to less than one year serve their time in the county jail. Counties also administer probation services for misdemeanants.

Administration: The CCPA grant program is administered by Probation and Parole Services in the Department of Corrections. The Assistant Secretary for Programs manages implementation of the act. The act did not authorize additional administrative funds or new staff. The primary role of staff is to review and process community correctional plans and provide technical assistance in the development of plans. The department is responsible for developing and monitoring minimum standards, policies, and administrative rules for the statewide implementation of the act. The department must report annually to the governor and the legislature on the effectiveness of participating counties in diverting nonviolent offenders from the state prison system.

Fundable Programs: Counties or groups of counties may request CCPA funds for:

- enhancement of county probation programs for jail-bound misdemeanants
- nonsecure residential drug treatment beds (360 statewide)
- construction and operation of a ninety-bed secure drug treatment facility
- construction and operation of a 256-bed work camp for prison-bound offenders (50 percent) and jail-bound offenders (50 percent)

The target group for residential facilities funded with CCPA monies is offenders who violate probation, parole, or community control (house arrest).

Application Process: Counties or groups of counties may compete to enter into a contract with the Department of Corrections for community corrections funds. In order to enter into a contract, a county must establish a correctional planning committee and must designate a county officer or agency to be responsible for administering community corrections funds received from the state. The county correctional planning committee must develop and implement a comprehensive five-year plan that includes descriptions of existing felony community corrections programs including restitution centers, a description of the new intermediate sanction to be provided, specific goals and objectives for reducing the number of commitments to the state prison system, evidence that net-widening will not occur, population descriptions of county-administered corrections programs for misdemeanants including detention facilities, descriptions of substance abuse treatment programs for offenders, an assessment of the need for additional programs, a projection of needs for the construction of county detention facilities and for diversionary programs, annual performance measures, and strategies for educating the public. The requests for contracts are to be reviewed by departmental staff, and final decisions are to be made by the Secretary of the Department of Corrections.

Funding Formula/State Appropriation: The legislature made specific appropriations for each type of program to be provided under the CCPA. There is no generic county funding formula. The legislature shifted $4.2 million from the Department of Corrections' community facilities budget to the non-secure residential drug treatment effort (360 beds statewide at $32/day per diem). The legislature appropriated $2.9 million for a ninety-bed secure drug treatment facility and a 256-bed work camp to be operated by the same county or group of counties. The legislature appropriated $150,000 to enhance county-administered probation services by providing additional intermediate sanctions.

Indiana Community Corrections Act

Purpose: In 1979, Indiana passed the Community Corrections Act. The purpose of the act is to divert offenders from incarceration at the state level and to encourage counties to develop a coordinated local system. The act targets the least serious felony offenders, misdemeanants, and juveniles.

Impetus/Leadership: In 1972, the General Assembly passed the Probation Subsidy Law, which required the state to subsidize 50 percent of the operating costs of the local probation programs. This program was never funded. In 1979, the Penal Code Commission, the Indiana Lawyers' Commission, and several private agencies joined together to lobby for a community corrections act. They promoted it to the General Assembly as a way of reducing the prison population by keeping appropriate offenders within the community, and as a humane alternative to incarceration. Once the act was passed, the Department of Correction joined the lobbying for funding.

Organizational Structure: The Indiana Department of Correction has three divisions: Administration, Operations, and Programs and Community Services. The Parole Section is located in the Programs and Community Services Division, while probation is a county function.

Administration: The Community Corrections Act is administered by the Division of Programs and Community Services of the Department of Correction. There are two full-time employees in the central office in charge of community corrections programs. Currently, they perform some field visits for purposes of observation and evaluation, provide consultation and technical assistance to counties in the development of community corrections plans, and review and approve applications for state grants. Personnel from other sections perform the other functions, such as fiscal audits. The staff plans to develop processes for auditing procedures and establishing minimum standards.

Fundable Programs: Community Corrections Act funds may be used to fund residential programs, work release programs, electronic house arrest programs, community service restitution programs, victim-offender reconciliation programs, jail services programs, jail work crews, juvenile detention alternative programs, and any other programs approved by the department.

Application Process: Participation in the Community Corrections Act is voluntary. The process begins with the county executive resolving to establish a community corrections advisory board. A group of counties may also combine to establish one board. The advisory board formulates the community corrections plan and the application for financial aid. A community corrections plan must include a description of each program for which financial aid is sought; the purpose, objective, administrative structure, staffing, and duration of the program; and the amount of community involvement and client participation in the program. Administrative regulations require that the plan include current expenditures for local corrections, estimated use of probation, the number of "executed commitments" to the DOC within the past calendar year, and the "impact relationship" between the project and current correctional needs in the jurisdiction. The county executive must approve the plan. The Division of Programs and Community Services reviews and approves the plans and applications and disburses the state funds.

Funding Formula/State Appropriation: Indiana developed a very complex funding formula based on population, population between the ages of ten and thirty-four, and net value of taxable property divided by total population. Although the department has simplified the calculations, the formula appears to be loosely followed. The department places the emphasis on the quality of the proposal and the needs of the county. The funds are distributed to the contracting agency 25 percent up front, with the balance being given in monthly reimbursements through the county.

A participating county is "charged back" 75 percent of the average daily cost of confining a person when an eligible offender is confined in a state correctional facility.

The Indiana General Assembly appropriated $15 million this biennium for community corrections programs.

Iowa Community Corrections Programs

Purpose: In 1973, Iowa passed legislation to create locally controlled community corrections programs. In 1977, the legislature adopted an organizational structure that mandated participation in the programs through judicial district organizations. The purpose of the community-based corrections system in Iowa is to provide nonincarceration sentencing options to the judiciary.

Impetus/Leadership: The impetus for enacting a system of community-based corrections programs in Iowa was two-fold. Criminal justice practitioners and legislators wanted to expand noninstitutional sanctions; they also wanted to move control of correctional programs from the state to local government.

Organizational Structure: The Iowa Department of Corrections is composed of the Division of Correctional Institutions, the Division of Community Correctional Services, the Division of Administration, and the Division of Prison Industries. The Board of Parole, an independent agency reporting to the governor, reviews adult felony cases in the state correctional facilities.

Administration: The Division of Community Correctional Services administers the community-based corrections program through eight judicial districts. Iowa is unique in that the state provides oversight for probation and parole services through contracts with judicial district organizations but does not provide services. The eight regional organizations are public agencies (similar to area mental health programs in North Carolina) that have local governing boards of directors. Agency staff are hired by the local boards.

The state staff in the Division of Community Correctional Services includes a director, deputy director, administrative assistant, field training officer, and data processing clerk. The state has regulatory responsibility for community corrections programs including technical assistance, development guidelines, accreditation, and funding.

Fundable Programs: Each of the eight local community corrections organizations is required to provide the following services: pretrial services, which screen and supervise defendants released from jail prior to trial; presentence investigations, which provide information to judges for sentencing decisions; regular and intensive probation services; residential facilities for prison-bound offenders, which provide twenty-four-hour supervision for an average of four to six months; parole supervision; work release facilities for prison inmates; and DWI residential facilities, which provide a ninety-day treatment program. There is no eligibility criteria for participation in community corrections programs.

Application Process: There is no application process for community corrections programs in Iowa. Funding for community corrections programs is part of the state budget process. The Department of Corrections distributes funds allocated by the legislature for community corrections programs through purchase of service contracts with the eight regional organizations. There is no requirement for submission of a local community corrections plan.

Funding Formula: Funds are distributed to the regional organizations based on work-load formulas for field services and residential services. In FY90-91, the legislature authorized $33 million for community corrections programs.

Kansas Community Corrections Act

Purpose: In 1978, Kansas passed a voluntary Community Corrections Act. The legislative intent of the act is to prevent the institutionalization of nonviolent offenders in state correctional institutions, though this is not clearly articulated in the statute. The mechanism for achieving this purpose is local correctional programs tailored to the needs of individual counties that contain at least one of two core services—intensive supervision or residential placement. In 1989, the Kansas legislature mandated participation of all counties in the Community Corrections Act.

Impetus/Leadership: The impetus for enacting a Community Corrections Act in Kansas came from the legislature. The legislature wanted to provide alternatives to both incarceration and to prison construction. The governor refused to sign the legislation and it became law without his signature.

Organizational Structure: The Department of Corrections administers adult institutions, community services, and parole services. The Supreme Court administers probation services.

Administration: The Community and Field Services Division of the Department of Corrections is responsible for oversight of community corrections programs. State staff provide technical assistance to counties, promulgate regulations, policies, and procedures, and audit program performance. In FY90, there were six staff involved in administering community corrections programs at the state level, with an administrative budget of $183,955.

Fundable Programs: The Community Corrections Act authorizes funds to be spent for planning and implementing community correctional services including, but not limited to, intensive supervision programs, restitution programs, victim services programs, presentence investigations, house arrest, residential programs, and community corrections centers.

The target population for these programs is first- or second-time convicted felony property offenders. However, no class of felony crime is automatically excluded.

Application Process: In order to apply for Community Corrections Act funds, counties or groups of counties must form a local corrections advisory board. The board develops a comprehensive local corrections plan. The application for CCA funds requires a description of offender target populations, prison admissions for the community, local sentencing practices, local prosecution practices, local revocation rates, local service analysis, and community demographics. The applicant must project the number of offenders who will be diverted from institutions, outline monitoring criteria, and demonstrate the ability to adhere to state minimum standards for community corrections programs. Staff review applications and, after consulting the State Community Corrections Board, recommend funding levels to the Secretary of the Department of Corrections.

Funding Formula/State Appropriation: Initially the Kansas Community Corrections Act used a formula developed in Minnesota for dispersing funds and required a chargeback to counties for certain felons who were incarcerated in the state prison system. The formula was intended to equalize funding available to different localities on the basis of their overall population, relative ability to support local correctional services, and relative burden or need for such services. The formula compared a county's "ability to pay" to the state average on the basis of per capita income and per capita adjusted property valuation. It measured relative need for services according to how a county's crime rate per 1,000 population and the size of its population aged five to twenty-nine compared to averages for the state. The formula averaged these four factors, and then they were multiplied by an annual appropriation factor, usually $5.00.

In 1989, the formula was amended and the chargeback was eliminated. The current funding formula is based on a per capita cost for each program service. For instance, in FY90, average per capita service costs were: adult intensive supervision, $1,510 per slot; adult residential services center, $42.85 per day or $15,640 per bed slot; presentence services, $134.00 per client served. In FY91, the legislature authorized approximately $10 million for community corrections programs.

Evaluation of the Act: In 1987, Temple University conducted a study of the Kansas Community Corrections Act. The study produced the following preliminary findings: (1) The CCA programs did appear to have drawn the majority of clients from a prison-bound population; (2) The reoffending rates among community corrections clients were no higher and no lower than would be expected of offenders with similar characteristics who are incarcerated instead; and (3) Community corrections programs handle offenders at a lower cost than incarceration. The researchers recommended revising the funding formula and reviewing the use of chargebacks to counties.

Michigan Community Corrections Act

Purpose: In 1988, Michigan passed a voluntary Community Corrections Act (CCA). The purpose of the act is to reduce crowding in state prisons and local jails by placing nonviolent offenders in safe, highly structured community punishment programs that do not jeopardize public safety. The act gives communities opportunities to assume responsibility and greater control over correctional programs and services provided to offenders.

Impetus/Leadership: Michigan legislators first began to explore the development of a Community Corrections Act to ease prison and jail crowding in 1980. During 1984-1988, a series of meetings and statewide seminars were held and an ad hoc task force was established to acquaint key leaders with the benefits of community corrections and to build consensus. Establishing a CCA was controversial because of philosophical and political differences. The Michigan Association of Counties and the Michigan Commission on Crime and Delinquency assisted legislators in building a consensus for the CCA. In 1988, the Michigan state legislature passed the CCA as a mechanism for reducing prison construction expenditures and a means of appropriately punishing nonviolent offenders in the community.

Organizational Structure: Adult institutions and the Adult Parole Board come under the jurisdiction of the Department of Corrections. The Bureau of Field Services in the Department of Corrections administers adult parole and felony probation services. The Department of Corrections is also responsible for monitoring local jails for adherence to state standards. The District Courts under the Supreme Court provide misdemeanant probation services. Misdemeanors serve active sentences in county jails.

Administration: The Office of Community Corrections administers the Community Corrections Act. It is an independent agency that is administratively housed in the Department of Corrections but does not report to the DOC in any way for policy matters. The office has a State Community Corrections Board appointed by the governor and confirmed by the senate. The Board provides oversight and policy authority for the office. This is a unique structure among the states that have CCAs.

There are fifteen staff in the Office of Community Corrections, including three grant coordinators who are assigned geographic areas of the state. The office provides technical assistance to counties or groups of counties in developing a local comprehensive corrections plan. In addition, the office reviews and approves local plans, enters into contractual agreements with local advisory boards for the operation of community corrections programs, monitors compliance with the agreements, and acts as an information clearinghouse. The annual administrative budget of the Office is approximately $1 million.

Fundable Programs: Counties or groups of counties may request CCA funds for:

- technical assistance grants: funds to assist local units of government to establish Community Corrections Boards and comprehensive local community corrections plans
- community grants: operational funds for a wide variety of community corrections programs including presentence diagnostic evaluations, pretrial intervention programs to reduce the jail population, highly structured nonresidential programs such as house arrest and day reporting centers, and a variety of types of residential programs
- minimum security jail work camps that emphasize community service work

CCA funds can not be used to replace current spending by local units of government for community corrections programs, for capital construction, or to create services which can already be obtained at the local level.

The emphasis for funds during the first year of operation of the act (1990) was on technical assistance to assist with the creation of local community corrections boards and the development of comprehensive plans. As the plans are completed, local communities will assume responsibility for the award and management of contracts for services. The current focus of local plans is to improve appropriate use of jail facilities and free up jail beds through the increase of pretrial release options. In addition, residential programs for prison-bound offenders are frequently included in local plans.

Application Process: In order to apply for CCA funds, counties or groups of counties must form local Community Corrections Boards. The Board must submit a comprehensive community corrections plan to the Office of Community Corrections to be approved. The office provides technical assistance grants to assist in this process. The local plans are very date-intensive and require analysis of the local offender population. The plans must describe various offender programs and services: what is currently being done, what needs to be done, and where scarce resources should be directed to more effectively address local correctional problems and needs. The plan must describe a system for the development, implementation, and operation of community corrections programs and an explanation of how the state prison commitment rate for the county, or counties, will be reduced, and how the public safety will be maintained. The data analysis must include a basic description of jail use, detailing such areas as sentenced versus unsentenced inmates, sentenced felons versus sentenced misdemeanants, and the use of a jail classification system. The analysis must include a basic description of offenders sentenced to probation and prison and a review of the rate of commitment to the state corrections system from the county for the preceding three years.

Staff from the Office of Community Corrections initially review requests for CCA funds based on objective criteria. Staff present recommendations to the State Community Corrections Board, which has final funding authority.

Funding Formula/State Appropriations: The legislature makes specific appropriations for various uses of Community Corrections Act funds. For FY92, the governor is asking for $956,000 for technical assistance grants, $13.5 million for Community Corrections Grants, $9 million for residential programs and $900,000 for minimum security jail work camps. CCA funds are distributed to local units of governments based on a formula. For technical assistance grants, the funding base for a single county is $40,000 and $15,000 for each additional county for a period of up to six months. For community corrections grants, the funding base is $20,000 for a single county community corrections board and $26,000 for each additional county. In addition to the base funding, counties are eligible for additional funds computed on the population of the county and the number of felony convictions.

Minnesota Community Corrections Act

Purpose: In 1973, Minnesota passed the Community Corrections Act. The act was proposed as a means of (1) providing more human services to offenders, and (2) reducing reliance on state institutions. The act targets a wide range of offenders: adult and juvenile, pretrial, postconviction, and postrelease. Counties tend to target their property offenders.

Impetus/Leadership: The community corrections movement began in one community when a group of local citizens and professionals joined together to discuss expanding local services to offenders. This resulted in the development of a residential unit as a local step between probation and prison. As more communities joined the movement, they pushed for a statewide act. The Department of Corrections joined in the effort as well. In 1973, the act was passed, and it began with three separate pilot programs.

Organizational Structure: The Department of Corrections is divided into two divisions: the Division of Institutional Services and the Division of Community Services. Counties under the Community Corrections Act assume the responsibility of providing probation, parole, and supervised release services for both adults and juveniles. In the remaining counties, felony parole services are provided by the state while probation services and jails are administered by the county.

Administration: The Division of Community Services in the Department of Corrections administers the Community Corrections Act. The Department has final approval of each county's annual comprehensive plan and budget. The department submits that budget as part of its appropriate package. Departmental staff act primarily as liaisons between the counties and the department, and between the counties and other counties. The staff also promulgates rules and provides technical assistance to the local boards to aid in the development of their comprehensive plans.

Fundable Programs: Community Corrections Act funds may be used for any felony program—pretrial, supervised release, or parole. Because of the increased use of local jails under the act, a portion of the state funds may be used for programs in jails, but not for jail construction.

Application Process: The application process for Community Corrections Act funds begins with a single county or a group of counties forming a community advisory board. This board, representative of the local community, develops an annual comprehensive plan and budget for the development, implementation, and operation of the community-based programs. The plan should be based on the needs and expenses of the local community. A comprehensive plan should include the manner in which presentence and postsentence investigations and reports for the district and juvenile courts will be made; the manner in which conditional release services to the courts and persons under jurisdiction of the commissioner of corrections will be provided; a program for the detention, supervision, and treatment of persons under pretrial detention or under commitment; delivery of other correctional services; and proposals for new programs, which must demonstrate a need for the program, its purpose, objective, administrative structure, staffing pattern, staff training, financing, evaluation process, degree of community involvement, client participation, and duration of the program. The board recommends this plan and budget to the board of county commissioners. Upon their approval, the plan is submitted to the Department of Corrections for final approval. During the process, the DOC reviews and revises the plan with the board members. The approved budget is submitted by the Department of Corrections as part of its appropriations request.

Funding Formula/State Appropriation: The funding equalization formula is based on the county's per capita income, net tax capacity, population at risk (age six through thirty years), and per capita correctional expenditures. The CCA funds are distributed on a quarterly basis. The legislature appropriated $24 million this year for community corrections programs.

A participating county is "charged back" a sum equal to the per diem cost of confining a juvenile in a state correctional facility. For adults confined in a state correctional facility, the per diem cost is deducted from the county's subsidy.

Impact Evaluations: In 1981, the Department of Corrections and the Minnesota Crime Control Planning Board released a ten-volume evaluation of the Community Corrections Act. They found that during the first five years of the act there had been significant improvement in local corrections planning and administration in CCA areas. They noted growth in the range and quantity of local corrections programming, and also a modest increase in the number of adult felons and a more substantial increase in the number of adjudicated delinquents (the target populations) retained in the community.

However, not all of the purposes of the act were attained. Public protection may not have been jeopardized, but neither had it been increased. The study also found that the act was not necessarily cost-effective. Although more "target offenders" were retained in the community in most CCA areas, not enough offenders were diverted from prison to offset the added administrative costs of the CCA.

Montana Community Sentencing Act

Purpose: In 1991, Montana passed a voluntary Community Corrections Act (CCA). The purpose of the act is to divert nonviolent felony offenders from prison. However, no funds were appropriated to implement the act. The act authorizes judges to order offenders into residential facilities for up to one year as a condition of a deferred or suspended sentence.

Impetus/Leadership: The impetus for the Community Corrections Act came from the legislature in response to prison crowding. The bill had been introduced previously but had not passed. Support was garnered from counties interested in operating residential diversion centers.

Organizational Structure: The Department of Corrections and Human Resources, renamed in 1991, administers adult institutions through the Institutions Section and felony probation and parole services through the Community Corrections Section.

Administration: The Community Corrections Act requires the Department of Corrections and Human Resources to develop administrative rules for community corrections programs with input from local communities. The department is authorized to contract with community corrections specialists to provide necessary technical assistance and training to judicial districts and corrections board.

Fundable Programs: Community Corrections Act funds, when appropriated, can be used only for residential diversion centers. Convicted nonviolent felony offenders are eligible for residential placement.

Funding Formula/State Appropriation: The legislature enacted the Community Corrections Act in 1991 but did not appropriate any funds to implement it. It is unclear, if funds are appropriated in the future, whether or not a funding formula will be used.

New Mexico Community Corrections Act

Purpose: In 1978, New Mexico passed a Community Corrections Act. The purpose of the act is to reduce the prison population. The act originally targeted both adult felons and adjudicated delinquents. In 1988, the Youth Authority was created and all juvenile community corrections programs were transferred to it. Now the act targets adult convicted felons in three categories: reintegration, diversion, and parole.

Impetus/Leadership: The Corrections Department led the way for enacting a Community Corrections Act as a means of reducing prison crowding. The act did not have any real force behind it until a series of prison riots in the early 1980s demonstrated the need.

Organizational Structure: The Corrections Department is responsible for all adult institutions and adult probation and parole services. The Corrections Commission advises the Secretary of the Corrections Department and participates in the policy-making process of the department. The Probation and Parole Division of the Corrections Department supervises all adult probationers and parolees.

Administration: The Adult Community Corrections Section of the Probation and Parole Division administers the adult Community Corrections Act. Staff from the division perform regular program and fiscal monitoring and auditing.

The act uses three levels of panels. The first level is the State Community Corrections Advisory Panel. This panel consists of criminal justice and community representatives. It makes policy recommendations, sets goals, and reviews all applications for funds and recommends them to the secretary. The second level is the State Selection Panel. This panel consists of departmental representatives who make the final acceptance or rejection of bids for services, and who recommend nonviolent felons to local selection panels for acceptance or rejection. The third level is the Local Selection Panel. This panel consists of volunteers at the local program level who screen referrals to the local programs. This panel recommends to the programs whether to accept or reject the offender.

Fundable Programs: Community Corrections Program funds may be used for diversion, reintegration, and parole programs. Examples include victim restitution, community service, job development, intensive supervision, family counseling, substance abuse programming, volunteer services, and residential services. The current emphasis is on reintegration programs through prisons and jails.

Application Process: The Corrections Department accepts bids for contracts based on the needs of the service area. The Probation and Parole Division determines the areas for programs based on the number of felons returning to their community who can be serviced there.

Counties, municipalities, and nonprofit organizations may submit proposals. Some form of an advisory board which is representative of that community must be in place. A proposal should include a description of the agency offering the proposal; the problem being addressed; a description of the target population; a description of the geographic boundaries of the service area; a program description including the goal statement, service components, service delivery policies and procedures, and the organizational chart; a work plan showing how the program will be developed and evaluated; and an indication of the community support for the program.

Funding Formula/State Appropriation: New Mexico does not use a funding formula; bids are accepted based on the needs of the communities. The Corrections Department establishes the service contracts and pays them out of the annual appropriation from the legislature.

The amount appropriated by the state varies with the number of contracts per year. The state appropriated $2.5 million for this fiscal year.

Ohio Community Corrections Subsidy Programs

Purpose: Ohio has implemented two community corrections subsidy programs: (1) a Community Corrections Act (CCA); and (2) the Community-Based Correctional Facilities and Programs Act (CBCFPA). The legislature enacted the Community Corrections Act in July 1979, and the Community-Based Correctional Facilities and Programs Act in April 1981. The purpose of both of these subsidy programs is to reduce the number of nondangerous offenders committed to state prisons and county jails by creating intensive correctional sanctions and services at the local level.

Impetus/Leadership: The impetus for enacting community corrections subsidy programs in Ohio was prison crowding. The legislature passed these subsidy programs in order to reduce commitments to the state prison system and to unify correctional services at the local level.

Organizational Structure: The Ohio Department of Rehabilitation and Correction administers adult state institutions and felony parole services. The Division of Parole and Community Services in the Department of Rehabilitation and Correction consists of the Adult Parole Authority, the Adult Parole Board, the Bureau of Community Services, and the Bureau of Adult Detention. The Adult Parole Authority may exercise general supervision over all probation officers in the state, including those in local probation departments. All parolees and certain probationers referred by the Court of Common Pleas on a contract basis are supervised by the Adult Parole Authority. In the remaining counties, probation services are provided by local probation departments. The Bureau of Community Services oversees the state's subsidy programs. The Bureau of Adult Detention administers the program to monitor and promote compliance with minimum standards for jails.

Administration: The Bureau of Community Services administers programs funded under the Community Corrections Act and the Community-Based Correctional Facilities and Programs Act. There are eleven staff at the state level to administer the community corrections subsidy programs with an annual administrative budget of approximately $350,000. State staff provide technical assistance to counties to apply for subsidy funds, develop program standards, and audit standards compliance and program performance.

Fundable Programs: Funds under the Community Corrections Act may be used for local probation service, parole services, preventive or diversionary corrections programs, release-on-recognizance programs, and specialized treatment programs for alcoholic and narcotic-addicted offenders. Funds under the Community-Based Correctional Facilities and Programs Act may be used for intensive probation supervision services and for residential services.

Application Process: To receive a state community corrections subsidy, counties or groups of counties must form a local corrections planning board. The board must submit a comprehensive plan for correctional services that demonstrates unified correctional services at the local level, the number of offenders who will be diverted from state or local penal institutions, and an ability to meet minimum program standards.

Staff review applications and recommend funding for programs on the basis of demonstrated need and satisfaction of specified priorities. Priorities for funds are established annually by the Department of Rehabilitation and Correction with advice from the State Community Corrections Advisory Board.

Funding Formula/State Appropriations: Based on appropriations made by the General Assembly, a minimum subsidy award is established that is supplemented based on the population of each county. In FY89, the legislature authorized $1,620,150 for Community Corrections Act Programs and $4,223,989 for programs funded under the Community-Based Correctional Facilities and Programs Act.

Evaluation of the Community Corrections Subsidy Acts: In 1989, the National Council on Crime and Delinquency evaluated the impact of Ohio's community corrections programs on public safety and costs. The study found that offenders placed in Ohio's community corrections programs had:

- been sentenced for serious crimes
- possessed lengthy criminal histories
- higher levels of program needs than traditional felony probationers. Profiles of offenders in the Intensive Supervision Probation Program and in residential programs indicated characteristics similar to offenders sentenced to prison for Class 3 and 4 determinate sentences.

The researchers concluded that Ohio's community corrections programs and, in particular, the Intensive Supervision Probation and residential programs, do divert offenders from prison. They found that the Community Corrections Act Program had less impact on diverting offenders from prison but it did, at a minimum, select the more serious cases typically placed on felony probation.

The study showed that rearrest rates for offenders placed in the Intensive Supervision Program and in residential facilities were well below a matched group of offenders sentenced to prison, and these programs produced a substantial savings in operational costs when compared to even short-term prison confinement. According to the researchers, these results indicated that carefully screened offenders can be diverted from prison to controlled community supervision without compromising the safety of the community.

Oregon Community Corrections Act

Purpose: In 1977, Oregon passed a voluntary Community Corrections Act (CCA). The purpose of the act is to provide sentencing alternatives and services for persons charged with criminal offenses.

Impetus/Leadership: The impetus for the Oregon Community Corrections Act came from the executive branch. In 1976, Governor Bob Straub's Task Force on Corrections proposed a new system of delivering community sanctions in Oregon. The task force recommended new legislation designed to "mobilize and facilitate a partnership of the best of both state and local services." In response to the task force's proposal, the 1977 legislature enacted the Community Corrections Act and provided state funds to enhance existing community programs and develop new sentencing alternatives to prison incarceration. By providing that each participating county be assessed a "payback" charge for each person sentenced for a class C felony, the legislature clearly implied that the control of the state's prison population was also a purpose of the CCA.

Organizational Structure: The Department of Corrections was created by the legislature in 1987. The department is responsible for the management and administration of adult corrections institutions, felony parole and probation services, and community corrections. The four branches are Administration and Planning, Community Services (probation and parole field services, community corrections programs), Inspections (jails), and Institutions (prisons). Historically, misdemeanor probation has been a county-funded and administered program. Under the Community Corrections Act, counties can also opt to provide felony probation services. All misdemeanants and felons sentenced to less than one year serve their sentences in local jails.

Administration: The Community Services Branch in the Department of Corrections administers both field services (probation and parole) and community corrections programs through a decentralized regional system. Along with field service responsibilities, state staff provide technical assistance in planning and implementing local community corrections plans. They also monitor program performance. State agency staff include an administrator, an assistant director, an executive assistant, four division administrators, and two community supervision administrators.

There is a state Community Corrections Advisory Board that advises the assistant director for corrections regarding program standards and rules. The board reviews local community corrections plans and recommends funding to the assistant director. The board is composed of fifteen members appointed by the governor.

Fundable Programs: The Community Corrections Act authorizes funds for nonresidential and residential programs and services including: (1) structured community sanctions for offenders; (2) drug and alcohol programs for at-risk offenders; (3) reentry programs for offenders leaving institutions; (4) preadjudication programs for persons in the criminal justice system; and (5) other alternatives to incarceration.

Though not explicitly stated in the legislation, the focus of CCA funds from the state perspective is to reduce the number of class C felons committed to the state prison system. Until 1989, the legislation included a payback provision that required counties to pay the state for each class C felon committed to the state prison system. The payback provision was amended numerous times over a ten-year period and was eliminated after it appeared to be an ineffective disincentive.

Application Process: In order to apply for CCA funds, counties appoint local community corrections advisory boards to plan correctional improvement and to determine how CCA funding should be spent. Counties submit applications demonstrating a need for the program, its purpose, objective, administrative structure, staffing, staff training, proposed budget evaluation process, degree of community involvement, client participation, and program duration. Applications are reviewed by the State Community Corrections Advisory Board and recommendations for funding are provided to the assistant director for Corrections.

Oregon has three options for participation in the CCA. Under Option I, counties get their full funding allocation, establish a community corrections board to draft the county's CCA plan, operate community programs and services funded with CCA funds, and take over responsibility for felony probation and parole from the DOC. Option I counties get the field services allocation for that county, which the DOC formerly used to operate felony probation and parole services. Thus, control of the field services allocation is the biggest incentive for counties to select Option I. Option II is the same, except (1) the county can contract with the DOC to continue to operate felony probation and parole, and (2) supervision fees are remitted to the DOC. In Option III counties, the DOC manages the community corrections process. The DOC's field services regional manager drafts a plan for use of CCA funds. He appoints a local advisory committee and asks them to comment on the plan. In addition, he sends a copy of the plan to the County Board of Commissioners, and gives them a chance to comment. Option III counties get 75 percent of the enhancement grant allocated to the county as well as 100 percent of the formula share of mental health and probation center funding. The state continues to operate felony probation and parole services.

Funding Formula/State Appropriations: Through the CCA, there are three pools of state aid for local community corrections programs: enhancement grants, mental health grants, and probation centers grants. Enhancement and mental health grants are allocated among counties using three equally weighted factors—each county's share of (1) the state's general population, (2) the population at risk (males and females between the ages of fifteen and twenty-nine), and (3) reported crimes, both misdemeanors and felonies. In the first biennium after the act was adopted, four probation centers were funded under the CCA. Because total probation center funding has not increased appreciably, no additional probation centers have been established under the CCA.

Until 1989, there was a payback from counties to the state to discourage class C felony commitments. When it was eliminated the payback was $3,000 per class C felony commitment to the state prison system. A ceiling limited the amount of payback each county was required to make over a two-year period. When the payback was in effect, the legislature had approved redistribution of these funds among participating counties that submitted approved supplemental plans. If a county lost $100,000 in paybacks, it could expect to gain $100,000 if its supplemental plan was accepted.

There has been a great deal of dissatisfaction over the formula for distributing CCA funds. Currently, the DOC is moving toward a workload formula for field services.

For FY91-93, the legislature appropriated $18,951,380 to counties for community corrections (field services, enhancement programs, mental health services, and probation centers).

Evaluation of the Act: Evaluations conducted from the late 1970s until 1983 suggested that the Community Corrections Act reduced the number of class C felony commitments compared to sentencing patterns that existed before the act. In a 1985 evaluation, research showed that class C felony commitments had been reduced by 1 to 3 percent per year since the CCA was passed. The evaluation failed to find significant differences in reductions among counties in the different options. Research conducted in 1986 by the Oregon Criminal Justice Council indicated that Option I counties sentenced a significantly lower percentage of Class C felons to prison than did Option II or III counties.

The researcher estimated that during the 1981-1983 biennium, reduction in prison commitments due to the CCA produced a total savings of 1,272 person/years. At the time, it cost about $14,264 to confine one inmate for a year. As a result, Carrow estimated that the CCA saved the state $18,143,800 in direct costs of confinement. During that time, it cost about $14,136,000 to fund CCA (not including field services). When adjusted for probation revocations, Carrow concluded that the

CCA cost about as much as it saved in reduced imprisonment costs.

Pennsylvania County Intermediate Punishment Act

Purpose: Pennsylvania enacted a County Intermediate Punishment Act in December 1990. The purpose of the act is to provide intermediate punishments for jail-bound offenders. The target population is nonviolent offenders who otherwise would be sentenced to county correctional facilities.

Impetus/Leadership: In response to prison crowding, Pennsylvania adopted revised sentencing guidelines in 1991. The guidelines were intended to reduce prison populations by shifting certain offenders to local jails. As a result, jails will become more crowded and the legislature enacted the County Intermediate Punishment Act to provide intermediate sanctions for jail-bound offenders.

Organizational Structure: The Department of Corrections operates state institutions for offenders, generally those sentenced to two years or more. County jails house offenders with active sentences of less than two years (generally). The State Board of Probation and Parole supervises offenders paroled from state institutions. County probation departments supervise misdemeanants and felons and parolees from local jails.

Administration: The Pennsylvania Commission on Crime and Delinquency administers the County Intermediate Punishment Act. The Commission is an independent agency that reports to the governor. Commission staff are responsible for reviewing local intermediate punishment plans, approving applications for funds, and developing and monitoring minimum program standards. The legislature did not appropriate any new funds to administer the act, so the Commission has absorbed this responsibility.

Fundable Programs: No state funds were appropriated to support the County Intermediate Punishment Act. A portion of the state's federal criminal justice grant money—Drug Control and Systems Improvement—was set aside to fund programs under the act. Fundable programs include (1) noncustodial programs that involve close supervision, but not housing, of the offender such as intensive supervision, victim restitution or mediation, alcohol or drug outpatient treatment, house arrest and electronic monitoring, psychiatric counseling, and community service, (2) residential inpatient drug and alcohol programs, (3) individualized services that evaluate and treat offenders, including psychological and medical services, education, vocational training, drug and alcohol screening and counseling, individual and family counseling and transportation subsidies, (4) partial confinement programs such as work release, work camps, and halfway facilities, and (5) alternatives to pretrial detention.

Application Process: In order to apply for Intermediate Punishment Act funds, counties or groups of counties must form a local board, which must submit a county intermediate punishment program plan to the Commission. Commission staff are available to provide technical assistance in the development of the plan. The plan must describe the number of nonviolent commitments to the county correctional facilities, population and existing conditions at the county correctional institution, local service capabilities, and involvement of the judiciary, criminal justice and correctional officials, and local government officials.

To apply for funds, counties must submit concept papers to the Commission on Crime and Delinquency. The concept paper must outline the proposed program, describe how it will affect on the county's correctional system, and describe evaluation strategies. Staff review the concept papers and recommend funding based on documentation of need.

Funding Formula/State Appropriation: There is no funding formula for programs funded under the County Intermediate Punishment Act. Grants are awarded on the basis of documentation of program services.

No state funds were appropriated to implement the County Intermediate Punishment Act. Instead, a portion of federal criminal justice funds administered under the Drug Control and Systems Improvement Grant Program was designated to support this new initiative. For FY91, $2.5 million was designated for these programs. Programs are eligible for a maximum of three years of funding and require matching funds: 25 percent local cash match the first year; 50 percent the second year; and 75 percent the third year. Construction and renovation projects are not fundable.

Tennessee Community Corrections Act

Purpose: In 1984, Tennessee passed a voluntary Community Corrections Act (CCA). The purpose of the act is to establish statewide community-based alternatives to incarceration for selected nonviolent offenders. The act provides resources between probation and prison so that more prison space is available for violent offenders.

Impetus/Leadership: The impetus for the Tennessee Community Corrections Act came from the legislature and the executive branch. In 1982, the State of Tennessee was placed under federal court order to reduce prison crowding. In 1985, the governor appointed a new commissioner of the Department of Correction and called a special session of the legislature to deal with prison issues. Recognizing the need for alternative constructive punishment, and to help reduce prison crowding, the Tennessee General Assembly passed the Community Corrections Act.

Organizational Structure: The Department of Correction is composed of the Adult Institutions Section, the Division of Community Services Section, and the Board of Paroles. Felons serve active sentences in the state prison system and misdemeanants serve active time in local jails. The Community Service Section oversees probation services, the Community Corrections Act, and standards for local jails. The state administers felony probation while the counties administer misdemeanant probation.

Administration: The Division of Community Services in the Department of Correction administers the Community Corrections Act. There are seven staff who manage the CCA grant program. They provide technical assistance to counties in the development of local community corrections plans. They review applications and make recommendations to the commissioner of Correction. Staff develop program standards and monitor compliance and program performance. In FY91, the legislature authorized $375,000 for administration of the CCA.

Fundable Programs: Counties or groups of counties may request CCA funds for alternatives to incarceration in jail or prison. These alternatives include noncustodial community corrections options that involve close supervision but do not involve housing the offender in a jail or workhouse. Programs include short-term community residential treatment options, residential in-house drug and alcohol treatment, and individualized evaluation and treatment services.

Only nonviolent prison- or jail-bound felony offenders are eligible for community corrections programs. State agency staff have developed two targeting instruments to assure that appropriate offenders are served in CCA programs. The Offender Profile Index (OPI) is a grid that predicts whether the offender is prison-bound based on current offense and prior criminal history. The Profile Index predicts the probability of incarceration based on comparisons with characteristics of prison inmates.

Application Process: To qualify for CCA funding, a county or group of counties within a single judicial district must establish a local Community Corrections Advisory Board. The board must submit a local community corrections plan to the Department of Correction. Recommendations for funding are based on documentation of (1) the number of nonviolent felony commitments to the Department of Correction, (2) population and existing conditions at the local jail, (3) rate of felony commitments per 1,000, (4) population of the judicial district and percent of population between the ages of eighteen and twenty-nine, (5) availability of local correctional services, (6) sufficient local service capacity to support the community corrections programs, and (7) demonstrated involvement and support from the judiciary, local criminal justice/correctional officials, and local government in the development of the community corrections plan. Staff rate applications using objective criteria and make recommendations to the commissioner of Correction.

Funding Formula/State Appropriations: There is no specific funding formula for individual CCA programs. Each approved program receives funds based on workload measures for the services they are rendering to offenders. In FY 90-91, the legislature authorized $5 million for Community Corrections Act Programs.

Texas Community Corrections Subsidy Programs

Purpose: In 1981, the State of Texas began subsidizing local community corrections programs by funding intensive supervision probation programs. In 1983, funds were authorized for restitution centers and court residential programs. Since then, an array of local community corrections programs have been added.

Impetus/Leadership: The impetus for subsidizing local community corrections programs in Texas was prison and jail crowding. The state has been under a federal lawsuit for a number of years, and the legislature authorized funds for community corrections programs in order to reduce commitments to state prisons and local jails.

Organizational Structure: The Texas Department of Criminal Justice has three divisions. The Institutional Division operates state institutions. The Pardons and Parole Division administers parole services for offenders released from the state prison system. The Community Justice Assistance Division established standards and provides funds for local community supervision and corrections departments. The 119 corrections departments are under the administration of the District Courts; probation officers are the employees of the courts. Local corrections departments are funded 50 percent by the state and 50 percent by counties.

Administration: Local community corrections subsidy programs are administered by the Community Justice Assistance Division of the Department of Criminal Justice. State staff provide technical assistance to counties to apply for subsidy funds, develop program standards, and audit standards compliance and program performance. In FY91, the legislature authorized $955,904 for administration of community corrections programs.

Fundable programs: State community corrections subsidies may be used for intermediate sanction programs including intensive supervision probation, electronic monitoring and house arrest, restitution programs, residential substance abuse facilities, court residential facilities, boot camps, community service programs, and day reporting centers. Funds are also provided statewide for pretrial release programs.

Application Process: In 1990, new requirements were added in order to receive subsidy funds for community corrections programs. Local corrections departments must form a local community justice council and must submit a community justice plan to the Community Justice Assistance Division. The plan must summarize existing services, describe new facilities or programs, describe the assessment process for placing offenders in the sanction, provide offender profiles of the target population, and outline an evaluation plan. There are separate pools of money for residential services, electronic monitoring, regular probation supervision, and a variety of intermediate sanction programs. Staff review applications and make funding recommendations based on funds available and the priority of the program in the jurisdiction's community justice plan. The Judicial Advisory Council, created in 1989, then reviews the applications and staff analysis before making its recommendations to the director of the Community Justice Assistance Division. The director presents recommendations to the Board of Criminal Justice for final approval.

Funding Formula/State Appropriations: Subsidies for probation supervision are allocated based on the number of officers supervising felony workloads. In 1990, the amount paid was $43,200 per officer. State funding for supervising misdemeanants averaged 62 cents per offender per day. Funds for other community corrections programs are also allocated by a workload formula. In FY91, the legislature authorized $62 million for probation supervision services, $20 million for residential services, $2 million for electronic monitoring, $2.5 million for risk assessment, $50 million for a variety of community corrections programs, and $5 million for discretionary grants.

Virginia Community Diversion Incentive Act

Purpose: In 1980, Virginia passed a voluntary Community Diversion Incentive Act (CDIA). The purpose of the act is to develop, establish, and maintain community diversion programs from prison and jail for nonviolent offenders who require more than probation supervision but less than institutional custody. The act seeks to give communities greater flexibility and involvement in responding to crime problems.

Impetus/Leadership: The impetus for enacting the Community Diversion Incentive Act in 1980 was prison crowding. The legislature, responding to recommendations from the executive branch, decided to expand the use of community sanctions in order to divert offenders from state prisons. Because of concerns about the impact on jail crowding, the act was amended in 1982 to include diversion from local jails.

Organizational Structure: The Department of Corrections is composed of the Division of Adult Institutions, the Division of Adult Community Corrections, and the Division of Administration. The Division of Adult Institutions oversees the State prisons, which house sentenced felony offenders. The Division of Adult Community Corrections administers felony probation and parole services, the Community Diversion Incentive Act, and inspection of local jails for meeting minimum standards. Virginia is unique in that the state funds 90 percent of operating expenses for jails and reimburses counties for construction of local jails.

Administration: The Division of Adult Community Corrections administers the Community Diversion Incentive Act. Staff within the division administer both probation and parole services and the CDIA. There are four regional administrators and twelve area managers who oversee probation and parole services and CDIA programs. In FY91, the legislature authorized $367,000 for administration of the CDIA.

Staff provide technical assistance to counties or private

providers who want to apply for CDIA funds. They review applications and make recommendations to the Secretary of the department. Staff provide oversight to the programs and monitor program performance.

Fundable Programs: The act authorizes CDIA funds to be spent for nonresidential and residential diversion programs and services. To date, all of the funds have been spent on intensive supervision programs. A variety of services are provided to offenders in these programs including, but not limited to, psychological testing and evaluation, counseling, basic education, vocational training, and residential placement. The only state-imposed service requirements are for case management, intensive supervision, and community service work. Offenders initially receive an active sentence; the CDIA program evaluates them for eligibility; they return to court, and the judge suspends the sentence if they voluntarily agree to intensive supervision. For offenders under intensive supervision, the CDIA Program may purchase other services including residential placement, counseling, and vocational training.

Application Process: In order to apply for CDIA funds, counties, cities, or groups of either must form local Community Corrections Resource Boards (CCRB). The CCRB applies for the grant funds and is responsible for operating, purchasing, or contracting for services approved in the application. Staff in the Division of Adult Community Corrections provide technical assistance in completing the grant application. Applications are reviewed competitively and are scored on (1) the experience and ability of staff to provide the programmatic services, (2) the adequacy of outlined programmatic services, (3) appropriateness and adequacy of policies and procedures, (4) financial condition of the agency as evidenced by an audit report, and (5) cost of providing the service. The applicant must specify the number of local misdemeanants, local felons, and state felons who will be diverted from jail and/or prison. The final funding decision is made by the director of the Department of Corrections.

Funding Formula/State Appropriations: Applicants request funds for core services and for offender services. The core service request can not exceed $50,000. The offender services budget is based on the number and type of offender who will be diverted from jail or prison: $4,200 per state felon, $700 per local felon, $4,200 per parole-eligible misdemeanant, and $300 for local misdemeanants. In FY91, the legislature authorized $10 million for the Community Diversion Incentive Act programs.

Evaluation of the Act: In 1985, the Virginia Joint Legislative Audit and Review Commission (JLARC) conducted an evaluation of the Community Diversion Incentive Program. The findings indicated that the Program is beneficial to the state in that it reduces the number of inmates incarcerated in correctional institutions and saves the state money.

According to the evaluation, CDI programs appeared to target an appropriate population. This determination was based on three tests. The first revealed that most state felons, local felons, and misdemeanants receive sentences of incarceration prior to referral to CDI. The second indicated that the majority of offenders who are evaluated for CDI participation but rejected are subsequently incarcerated. The third indicated that a large number of state felon divertees statistically resemble the incarcerated population. The report noted that judicial discretion and varying sentencing practices and philosophies of judges make it difficult for the DOC to totally control the population in CDI and therefore the majority, but not all, of the clients in the program would have been incarcerated.

According to the findings, the CDI Program saved the state an estimated $325,461 for FY84, though this may be a conservative estimate of the savings generated. To strengthen the cost-savings nature of the program, it was recommended that the director of the DOC undertake an intensive assessment of the CDI population in order to determine the types of offenders who should and should not be diverted.

The program had been operating a short period of time when the study was conducted, so recidivism and repeat offense rates of CDI divertees could not be comprehensively assessed. Of the offenders who had been successfully terminated from the program when the study was conducted, 3.9 percent had been convicted of a new offense. The report noted that the DOC needs to strengthen its recidivism tracking system in order to assess the impact of the program.

About the Author

Mary K. Shilton, J.D., is assistant director at the National Association of Criminal Justice Planners in Washington, D.C., where she is responsible for conducting research on developments in criminal justice agencies and has participated in research and analysis of the National Judicial Reporting System's study of probation in 32 jurisdictions. In addition, as a member of the advisory board of the Alexandria Detention Center in Virginia, she has helped develop a volunteer female offender education program and has performed a variety of advisory functions on management issues for the jail. She received her juris doctor degree from the University of California's Hastings College of Law in 1974 and a master's degree in corrections, youth, and social policy from the University of Oregon in 1971.